Appointment With Destiny
Real Life Case Histories

by Katherine de Jersey
Author of *Destiny Times Six*
with Isabella Taves

J & B Editions, Inc.
Publishers

For information write:
J & B Editions, Inc., Publishers,
3113 W. Marshall St., Suite 1G,
Richmond, VA 23230.
To order additional copies of *Appointment With Destiny*,
call 1-800-266-5480.

Book Design by Jan Carlton and Bob Friedman
Edited by Jan Carlton
Cover Design by Jamie Raynor
Illustrations by Eliza B. Askin
Computer Astrological Charts prepared
by Eleanor Haspel-Portner,Ph.D.

10 9 8 7 6 5 4 3 2 1

Printed in the United States of America

For RPG

who taught me how to live, to love, to laugh!

TABLE OF CONTENTS

FOREWORD

At the time I became interested in astrology, information about it as a serious subject required a commitment of time as well as intent because the popularized notion of astrology did not reflect the true science of the subject. As a social scientist, I wanted to understand how and if astrology had something to offer a true explorer of consciousness and personality. I had studied astrology for a couple of years on my own, finding it the most complex field I had ever encountered. Thus, when I had an opportunity to have Katherine de Jersey do my astrological chart, I looked forward to the experience with great anticipation.

My initial analysis with Katherine overwhelmed me; she has skill beyond what I could comprehend from my studies. From the chart she drew up, she knew all kinds of intricacies of my personality and my life that even the best designed personality test in the hands of a truly gifted psychologist could not have mapped out. I wanted to understand more of what Katherine did and I wanted to know more of what she could see in the charts. I began an exploration with her that has continued to grow over the years. Initially, I had her do charts for my children; I put the tapes away for more than ten years before I played them for my children. They were astounded at the accuracy of the map Katherine had made of the events as well as of the psychological climate of the various times in their lives.

Through Katherine I have come to understand the way astrology can be used constructively and have observed many dabblers in astrology who misuse it and its potential for information. Katherine can see in a chart what the forces acting upon a person present to that person; she can see the timing of the energies as they approach and grow stronger and she can see the timing of the energies as they weaken and move away. An individual who is aware and sensitive to the energies of the cosmos acting upon them both internally and externally, can transcend the physical dimension and transform the level on which manifestation occurs.

Every individual has positive forces as well as negative ones which help them grow in awareness of themselves; by using the astrological road map, Katherine helps individuals anticipate the forces as they will impact them and move through them with less stress. For example, when I planned to move to California, I wanted to time my move for the least stress; Katherine and I talked at length about the factors in my chart at the time. The financial stress factors were there; I decided with her help that because they were there regardless of what I did I may as well move and be working toward something I wanted rather than staying in a place that was not my true "home." It did help me, however, to know that after a certain time the fog would lift and the stress would no longer be in the financial area.

Proper language in astrology can make a world of difference in the accuracy and in the nuance of its communication. Katherine is a master at this language; she does not use aspects in astrology as immutable forces as so many astrology students do. She sees aspects and expresses them as energies which have subtle influences on the consciousness

8

of action patterns in an individual living a life. She uses her language skill to express to these individuals, as much as language can, what to expect from these energies so that the individual can master his own life free of the forces of the universe but very much in tune with them.

Working with Katherine for twenty years has given me great respect for the astrological field as well as for her in her skill as a master of the astrological tools. My life has been richer because of Katherine who has contributed valuable insights to me and my family; my psychological practice has been enriched by having Katherine as a resource who has contributed by the use of astrology to the depth of the work I can do with my clients.

The cases Katherine presents in this book show only some of what astrology can do in the hands of those skilled in its tools. The cases weave the fascinating web of interplay between the road map of fateful forces and the power of individual freedom to change those energies to create one's own destiny.

Eleanor Haspel-Portner, Ph.D.
Clinical Psychologist
Pacific Palisades, California
November 1, 1994

INTRODUCTION

Are you a skeptic? Do you think astrology is non-sense? Horoscopes are amusing, but that's all? Listen to Henry Miller, one of the most brilliant writers of our time:

"Astrology does not offer an explanation of the laws of the universe, nor why the universe exists. What it does, to put it in simplest terms, is to show us that there is a correspondence between macro-cosm and microcosm. In short, that there is a rhythm to the universe, and that man's own life partakes of this rhythm.

". . .A chart when properly read should enable one to understand the overall pattern of one's life. It should make a man more aware of the fact that his own life obeys the same rhythmical, cyclical laws as do other natural phenomena. It should prepare him to welcome change, constant change, and to understand that there is no good or bad, but always the two together in changing degrees, and that out of what is seemingly bad can come good and vice versa. Astrology might indeed be called a science of relating, whose first fruit is the dictum that fate is character."

Do you say about astrology, "Very interesting, but what about the scientists — they don't believe in it, do they?"

Listen again: this time to Frank A. Browne, Jr., who was until his retirement Morrison Professor of Biology at Northwestern University, whom I heard

11

lecture for the Radio Engineers' Club of America several years ago, and with whom I had the privilege and honor of sharing the microphone on TV.

"Links have now been securely forged between living organisms and the fluctuating electromagnetic forces of their environment. We cannot gainsay that the living organism is as sensitive a receiving system as the composite of all of man's artificial electronic equipment by which he gains geophysical and astrophysical information. Geophysicists are now busily unraveling the multiplicity of ways in which variations in these atmospheric forces are related to the activities and movements of the earth, sun, moon, and planets, and even the distant stars. Now, tied to their continuing discoveries are the paralleling, inescapable questions of possible biological significances."

This writer has studied and practiced astrology for more than thirty years, which means I have only begun! It is a very complex and fascinating study. Astrology is both a science and an art, and requires the type of mind that combines the two. Medical astrology is a field all its own and it must be studied in depth by an open mind, such as that of the physician who introduced me to astrology as he researched the cause(s) of cancer.

This book was written to show what *real* astrology is, what it can do, and how it can help us to better understand and direct our lives to get the most out of them — *AND* put the most *INTO* them!

UNDERSTANDING? TIMING? RELATIONSHIPS? These are probably the three most important areas of our lives, the three that trouble us the most. And only astrology really gives the answers — at least, many of them. So what is astrology? It is the study of the response of life on earth (or in space) to the electromagnetic fields emanating from the sun, the moon, and the planets, and the angles formed among them at any given moment, at any specific place (the precise latitude and longitude) on the earth.

And what is a horoscope? It is a mathematically calculated chart or map of these planetary positions. It is *not* fatalistic, it does *not* predict specific events — merely the *trends*.

For further explanation, I suggest you consult some of the excellent books written by our master astrologers — there are many. However, it is for you to learn to discriminate between the *true* and the *false* — genuine and fake — as it is in every area of life! Give it a try — I did — and I'm glad.

It is interesting to note that the nature of relationships is changing. As we have become more and more aware of the changing times — in morals, money, interests, attitudes toward sex — so does it seem that people are changing their relationships. What they desired before, in the way of love affairs, or in friendships, does not seem to be appropriate now. Or, it is not what we want. Why? — because people are changing, of course. And so we should not expect what we found so desirable before to be fulfilling now! And perhaps not next year. Probably the best way we can estimate what we'll find exciting, or at least interesting, in the next few years is to take an in-depth perspective of ourselves. At what stage are we in our personal lives?

A striking example of the change taking place in what the general public wants is the growing number of talk shows, and the obvious wish of so many of the guests to discuss their intimate relationships in public, and to indulge their egos by taking over center stage on TV!

Will this public airing help us to relate happily to others close to us? Or, will it serve to cheapen some relationships by exposing ourselves to public opinion and further strain the relationships?

Would an in-depth study of astrology help everyone to better understand each other? It should, unless it is misused, by reading into the charts only what the individual wants to see!

To me, astrology is a never-ending adventure into the mysteries of life. It has opened up new worlds of understanding and insight into the intricacies and complexities of life. To quote Marlon Brando in his recent interview with Larry King, "after all, we have to look inward before we look outward, don't we?"

When astrology is interpreted correctly, it provides a detailed map of the hows, wheres, and whys of a person's inner being. Actually, an individual's chart is a blueprint to the soul___ and the heart.

To most of us, relationships are probably the most important aspect of life. Only astrology reveals the true nature of the connections and the secrets of the subconscious. Even a psychotherapist can learn through exploration of the chart, and many psychologists are using astrology today.

Timing is another important aspect of life. Again, astrology is the answer. Change is the only constant in life. Although changes may seem erratic, they actually evolve through the cycles and the rhythm of the universe. There is a time to begin and a time to finish, whether it be a relationship, a career, or a business. A personalized chart will tell a person when.

There are certain basic principles to the way I conduct my astrological practice.

#1 Never take one planetary aspect out of context of the whole pattern of the chart. It is the combination of all the planetary influences at a precise moment in time at a specific place that gives us the complete

picture. Correct interpretation is the art of synthesis.
#2 Never make a flat prediction. The further we progress in life, the more we realize that there are choices! The astrologer should explain the choices and make suggestions. The chart should be used as a guide to make decisions, not as a final dictum.

#3 Astrologers should always strive to give a positive message with specifics. Most people come to an astrologer when they are troubled. So we must guide them with the whens, whys, hows, and what to do about it. Astrology gives a perspective, as it can open up new worlds for the client. It helps us to see the positive side of every person and situation. And above all, it reminds us of the importance of attitude____ that what happens is not really what counts, but how we react to it!

We cannot change the past, nor avoid the future, but we can control our reactions! That is the secret of life! If we are not too serious about life and ourselves, life can be a wonderful game — and with that thought in mind, we can't lose, can we?

Katherine de Jersey

A SHAKESPEARIAN TRAGEDY IN LOS ANGELES
THE DOWNFALL OF A SPORTS ICON

On July 9, 1947 a handsome little boy was born in San Francisco at 8:08 a.m., Pacific Standard Time.

On May 19, 1959, in Rollenwald, Germany, near Hamburg, a beautiful blond girl was born at 4:44 p.m., Central European Time.

He was destined to become a hero in the eyes of the world — a champion football star, a talented actor, a magnetic personality.

She grew up to become a beauty, adored and desired by men wherever she went.

Early on the morning of June 13, 1994, a neighbor, alerted by a distraught white Akita wandering without a leash, found two people brutally murdered — a young man and a blond woman with her throat slashed so deeply it was almost severed. They were killed in front of the town house condominium owned by Nicole Brown Simpson, who had been recently divorced from the famous O.J. Simpson, winner of the Heisman Trophy and a legend in football history.

Indeed, she was one of the victims and the other was a twenty-five-year-old waiter named Ronald Goldman, who apparently *just happened* to be there, returning prescription dark glasses which Nicole

Simpson had inadvertently left the evening of June 12 at the restaurant where he worked. The two were on the doorstep of her condo when they were attacked.

Police found two small children, a girl and a boy, asleep upstairs, and took them to the police station where they sat bewildered with coloring books and crayons. Then cops went in search of O.J. Simpson whose Brentwood estate was a short distance from the home of his ex-wife. They rang the intercom but could rouse no one. Seeing what could have been a spot of blood on the white Bronco they thought parked carelessly on the street, and fearing harm might have also come to the football star, one cop leaped the fence, where he stumbled upon a blood-stained brown glove, apparently the mate of the one that had been found at the murder scene. He opened the gate for the other police who roused Arnelle Simpson, twenty-five, O.J.'s daughter from a previous marriage, who had been sleeping in one of his guest cottages. She let them into the house and called Simpson's personal assistant who had been with him for twenty years, to find out the whereabouts of her father.

It turned out that he had been scheduled to attend a golf outing in Chicago on June 13, to help entertain the guests of Hertz-Rent-A-Car, his sponsor. He had caught the red-eye flight from Los Angeles International Airport and arrived in Chicago at 6:15 a.m., local time. A few hours later, the police called and told him his ex-wife had been murdered. He immediately took the next plane back to L.A. Then began five days of melodrama, culminating in the famous chase of Friday, June 17, which preempted television shows across the nation. Millions of people watched O.J. Simpson sitting in the white Bronco being chased down the freeway with twenty-five police cars in pursuit.

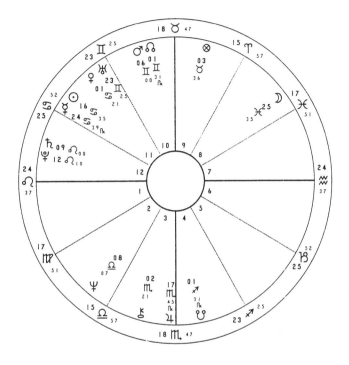

O.J. Simpson
Jul 9 1947   8:08 AM PST
San Francisco   California
37N47   122W25
Jul 9 1947   16:08:00 GMT
Tropical   Placidus   True Node

It was a scene out of a Hollywood movie. O.J. was to surrender to police before noon. Unbeknown to most people, Simpson had been staying with his friend, Robert Kardashian, all week. O.J.'s new lawyer, Robert Shapiro, had gone to Kardashian's home to be with him when O.J. surrendered to police. To Shapiro's dismay, O.J. and Al Cowlings, another close friend, skipped out the back door of the lower level of the house and departed in the white Bronco while he, Shapiro, was on the top level

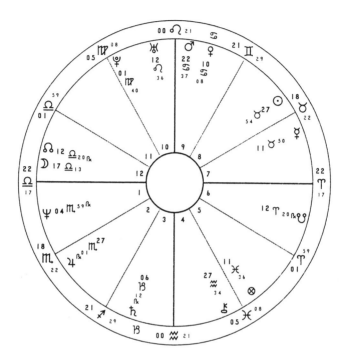

Nicole Simpson
May 19 1959   4:44 PM CET
Hamburg   Germany
53N33   9E59
May 19 1959   15:44:00 GMT
Tropical   Placidus   True Node

in the front of the house.

With Simpson's departure, police put out a bulletin for his arrest. Hours passed. The Bronco was finally located speeding down the expressway with Simpson, a gun to his head, sitting in the back seat threatening to commit suicide while Cowlings talked to the police, telling them his friend wanted to kill himself on the grave of his ex-wife. Persuaded to return home, Simpson called his mother. Then he surrendered quietly and was taken to the police sta-

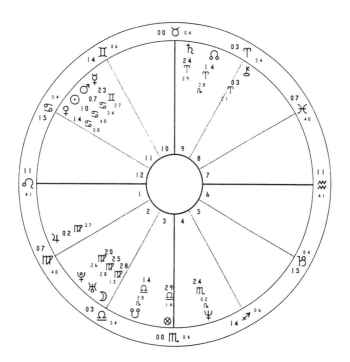

Ronald Goldman

Jul 2 1968   8:00 AM CDT
Chicago   Illinois
41N51   87W39
Jul 2 1968   13:00:00 GMT
Tropical   Koch   True Node

tion where a suicide watch was kept on him for several days.

I was as spellbound as anyone else watching the chase, which seemed almost surreal as other cars pulled off to the side of the interstate and pedestrians cheered, "Go, go Juice." The astrologer in me had to know what was going on and why. I found O.J.'s birth date — July 9, 1947, in San Francisco — in my celebrity register and set out to calculate his chart. I didn't put it aside until I figured that the time of

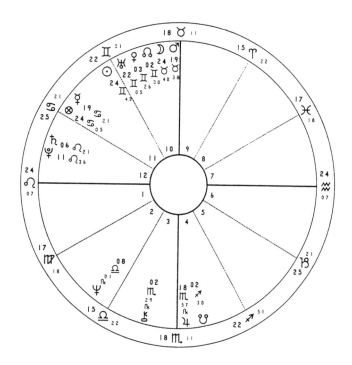

Al Cowlings

Jun 16 1947	9:36 AM PST
San Francisco	California
37N47	122W25
Jun 16 1947	17:36:00 GMT
Tropical	Placidus	True Node

his birth was 8:08 in the morning. Later I learned his birth certificate confirmed this time.

He has his sun in Cancer and moon in Pisces, the two most sensitive signs in the zodiac, and was known for his kindness and consideration of busboys, waiters, and people in service, as well as for his charm and warmth to teammates. Leo was on the ascendant, making him the actor and athlete combined. His birth date was close to the powerful fixed star Regulus, and he was graced with striking good looks — an air of aristocracy and style. The sad corollary of this is that he was driven to be the best, to have the most, in every department of life. He looks like a tribal chief — born in the wrong century in the wrong country. When the Buffalo Bills traded him as he grew older, despite his spectacular career, he was deeply hurt. And when his beautiful blond wife, whom he adorned with every possible luxury — he bought $60-a pair stockings for her and they had his-and-her identical white *Ferraris* — rejected him, it was more than he could accept.

They were presumably very much in love, a beautiful couple. Whether he really loved her, or whether he needed to possess her as a prize, is a question. At any rate, to a man of his sensitivity, who consorted easily with white people, whom his sponsor, Hertz, regarded as a person who transcended color, who was accepted in white circles, the idea of losing her to the white men she dated after the divorce was more than he could handle.

I went to bed still thinking about O.J. I couldn't get him out of my mind. The next day, I called Albert Clayton Gaulden, an astrologer in Arizona whom I have known over the years, and discovered he was as fascinated as I. Starting July 3 I was due to attend an astrologers' convention in Anaheim, California where I was to present a lecture. I told him what I had found in O.J.'s chart and gave him the birth date. He was eager to make his own calculations and we agreed to work together on a joint presentation at the convention.

Careful study of Nicole's and O.J.'s charts indicates the trial is likely to drag on for a long time. Both the prosecution and the defense may spring surprises. I believe he killed her — *it had to be*. There is indication the trial will go into 1995.

O.J. Simpson was a generous man. He supported his mother, his two grown children from a first marriage, and was extremely good to Nicole's family. He was able to get a Hertz dealership for her father, he put her cousin in charge of one of his Frontier Chicken restaurants, and he sent her sister Dominique to the University of Southern California. But, although he nurtured the ones he cared about, he also controlled them. When he was rebuffed by anyone he helped, he engaged in a classic pattern of anger and rage triggered by fear of abandonment and rejection. His usual manner for all the world to see is engaging. On television, he was disarming, friendly, seemingly at peace with himself, and pleased to be O.J. Simpson. But a darker side lies just below the mask.

As any life unfolds, it becomes a gradual maturing process. This is particularly true of Cancerians. For many, this growth is good, but gradual. Unfortunately for O.J., the potential evil beneath the surface grew also, but he was able to hide this from the public. Leo is his rising sign — he is the performer, the world's a stage and he is the star on it.

His deep attachment to his mother explains why, although he dated many attractive women, the two women he married could never live up to his expectations. His first marriage was to a former schoolmate who gave him three children, Arnelle, Jason, and Aaren, a twenty-three month old girl, who died in a tragic swimming pool accident a few months before his divorce from his first wife. He met Nicole in 1974 when she was a waitress at The Daisy, a popular night spot in L.A. She moved in with him before his divorce. And he was so infatuated with her, he insisted she quit community college to accompany him on his many out-of-town trips. They married in 1985 and had two children, a girl, Sydney, nine on October 17, 1994, and a boy, Justin, six. When he was elected to the Pro-Football Hall of Fame, he made a graceful speech, crediting Nicole with bringing him his greatest happiness at a tragic time in his life, his retirement from football.

Romance? A great love? That's not the way the romance is described in their charts. Infatuation? Yes! Obsession? Yes! A powerful sexual attraction? Of course! But that is not enough to last forever unless there is unselfish love, which obviously they didn't have. Perhaps what they were finding in each other was a substitute for love. Sex is beautiful and essential in a relationship, but it is not enough when self-love is stronger. Then it turns into greed for self-satisfaction.

Nicole's craving for attention and O.J.'s need for always being center stage destroyed the mutual love that could — and should — have been the center of their lives and preserved their marriage. Actually, the racial difference, which could have been analyzed and made a source of strength between them, was probably more of a problem than they ever realized. They should have had in-depth analysis together. Therapy might have prevented the tragedy.

Obviously, O.J. had to be king, controlling the situation, and Nicole had to be queen, garnering plaudits from the world around her. And neither would accept less. That meant trouble between them. Born with her sun in Taurus, Nicole could never get enough love and adoration, and neither could he. And their substitutes for love and adoration were material things — beautiful, expensive cars, clothes, and impressive houses.

Actually, she loved him more than he loved her. She was crazy about him! She had Venus, the planet of love, conjunct Mars, the planet of sex, in Cancer, indicating very strong love. He had Mars in Gemini amd Venus in Cancer — sometimes this is the womanizer, a man whose self-love is paramount.

Her planet Jupiter opposed the sun, warning of over-indulgence and extravagance in material things. She was vain, flirtatious, and worked hard on her body to keep it young and desirable. After the divorce, she picked up with a group of aspiring actors — among them Ronald Goldman who was marking time as a waiter — and partied with them like any twenty-five-year-old, sharing her *Ferrari* and picking up checks at night clubs.

The bitter jealousy Simpson and Nicole both suffered is seen in their charts, indicating a special tragic karma or fate. For Nicole, I have seen the same aspects in the heavens at her birth as those in the chart of the Russian Czar Nicholas II (bizarre, the similarity of the two names), who was murdered in 1918. Both had their sun in the Pleiades (a group of fixed stars, often troublesome) at birth. Nicholas was beheaded and Nicole's head was nearly severed. Incidentally, Isadora Duncan, the famous American dancer at the turn of the century, who was beheaded in an automobile accident by her long trailing scarf, also had a degree of death in the Pleiades. The actress Jayne Mansfield also shared this degree. (*This does not apply to everyone born at this time!*)

Actually, Simpson, despite his penchant for pretty women, was never a ladies' man. He played around, yes, but at heart he was a man's man, popular with his teammates and close to two male friends, Al Cowlings and Robert Kardashian. After the chase, Cowlings was charged by the angry police for "harboring a fugitive." Later the charges were dropped for the time being.

Al Cowlings, born the same year as O.J. but about a month before, June 16, 1947, with the sun in

Gemini, is like O.J.'s second self, reflecting his personality. Indeed, they were best friends in the tough section of San Francisco where they were born, and played star backs together at Galileo High School. Al went with O.J. to San Francisco College and later to the University of Southern California. Simpson was always the star, prodding Al to keep up his grades. When Simpson was picked by the Buffalo Bills, where he starred spectacularly for years, he saw to it that Al was drafted into the organization.

By the same token, when in the twilight of his career Simpson was traded to the San Francisco 49ers, Al followed him. And in later years, when Al found the financial sledding rough, O.J. hired him as his six-foot-five, two hundred forty-five pound bodyguard and stand-in for movies.

Kardashian, while his background with Simpson does not go quite so far back as Al's, has been a close friend in Simpson's social life, almost like a family member. Simpson saw him through a painful divorce and now, as Kardashian is planning to be married again, he has put the wedding on hold to be with Simpson. Every day he visits him in his cell. There have been rumors, unsubstantiated of course, that Kardashian had something to do with the disappearance of a duffle bag which might have contained the bloody clothes O.J. discarded after the murders.

Al Cowlings has been silent and speaks only through his attorney. They insist he knows nothing of the passport and almost $10,000 in cash police found in the Bronco after the police confiscated it. For a month, he was free on bail of $250,000 before the charges were temporarily dropped and bail money returned. The close friendship between the two men makes it impossible to think that O.J. would not tell him he was trying to escape.

O.J.'s chart indicates he had an accomplice in this tragedy. The explosive planetary aspect which showed the sudden volcanic eruption of O.J.'s nervous system was in the sign of Gemini and Sagittarius, which are dual in nature and usually involve two. They would suggest that O.J. had some kind of help in a cover-up. This planetary influence was in the fifth and eleventh houses which represent friends and children.

So far as I am concerned, careful and thorough study of Nicole's and O.J.'s charts convinces me that O.J. was capable of the violence which left the two bodies in pools of blood. I calculated the diurnal chart (a chart for the day) for O.J. of the murder date, June 12, 1994. *Using his specific birth data, it sets the stage for the events of that day and night in his life and his life only.* There is the tone of violence, suffering, and uncontrolled passions, resulting in O.J.'s ending up a very isolated and *lonely* being before he realizes how he really needs others!

He seeks recognition but likes to show he doesn't need it. Therefore, we observe the arrogance with which he walks off without really showing gratitude for the applause. He exhibits a keen sense of rivalry and competition (*he thought he won this one*) but a lack of sportsmanship (to put it mildly!). Will this attitude lead to his downfall? Nonetheless, his persona may never cease to amaze and intrigue his public!

On May 20, 1947, less than a month before his birth, there was a total solar eclipse at twenty-eight degrees of Taurus, the fixed star in the Pleiades. It was right on Nicole's sun — ominous! This eclipse recurred May 19, 1985, on her birthday, the year they were married. Talk about fate! Karma that could not be denied — set before birth. I charted the days when Nicole called 911 to report violence, September 11, 1983; January 1, 1989; and October 25, 1993, and I recognized the planetary aspects similar to the ones I saw in the pre-birth charts. This to an astrologer is like finding the fingerprints of the same culprit at different crimes.

The attacks on Nicole varied in intensity. The one on New Year's Day got O.J. fined with a demand that he consult a psychiatrist and do a certain number of hours of public service (which he got out of by saying he had done more public service than anyone in the courtroom). But all of the attacks were a rehearsal for the night of June 12, 1994.

In the previous nights of violence, he was almost angry enough to kill her, but not quite. When he finally realized that he was never going to get her back — he admitted this earlier the same evening when he had dinner with his house guest, Brian (Kato) Kaelin — the rage became too powerful to resist. The drama became too exciting; he could not stop — he was completely out of control!

He had come under the spell of his darker side, the side he does not acknowledge. It was like the Jekyll-Hyde syndrome, he became another person. Even the New Year's quarrel where he left Nicole so badly battered, he brushed off as, "One of those family spats, it happens to everybody." It was a typical O.J. reaction — he simply closed his mind to the matter — the same kind of concentration of focusing in a certain direction that enabled him to attain his goals.

Is that why he can sit in court looking so calm, smiling at his daughter Arnelle when she leaves the stand, enduring his incarceration in a small cell because he believes in his own innocence? He is convinced he is not the man who beat his wife brutally, not the man who committed the two bloody murders. There was a powerful negative aspect from Pluto in his chart at that time. It may be that he was under the influence of drugs which released the dark side of his nature until he became crazed, unable to stop the butchery, and getting sexual satisfaction from the awful acts — a side that he does not acknowledge.

The strong point in his chart is Jupiter in Scorpio, which describes his loving relationship with his mother — the most beautiful aspect in his chart. His Grand Trine in the intuitive water signs (Scorpio, Cancer, and Pisces) represents the love and spiritual strength which is one part of his complex nature — multiple personalities. Saturn joined to (conjunct) Pluto in the twelfth house, darkens his moods and overpowers the good in him. Part of him is beautiful and, unfortunately, part is *evil*!

I kept pondering the possibility of O.J. having multiple personalities and decided to call my friend in Los Angeles, Eleanor Haspel-Portner, Ph.D., a well respected psychologist and author of *Marriage In Trouble: Time of Decision*, to discuss the likelihood of such a condition. She stated that she believed he did not have a multiple personality disorder. If he did he would be less predictable and would experience lapses in time, reflecting a more visible shift in personality. Also, multiple personality disorder patients tend to be nonviolent toward others. Nor did she believe him to be schizophrenic. "To be schizophrenic, he would be less charming and verbal in his manner, using some odd patterns of speech, more aloof and somewhat withdrawn in his demeanor.

"To a trained observer," Eleanor explained, "he seems to be more of a narcissistic personality. These types of people are very highly functional — they see people with whom they have a relationship as a possession. Any hurt from this person, real or imagined, can put them into a rage. They tend to be split off from their feelings.

"With narcissistic personality disorder, the essential feature is a grandiose sense of self-importance or uniqueness, as well as preoccupation with fantasies of unlimited success, an exhibitionistic need for constant attention and admiration, and characteristic responses to threats to one's self-esteem. Characteristically, in narcissistic personalities, disturbances in interpersonal relationships often alternate between extremes of over-idealization and devaluation."

Eleanor went on to say, "Individuals with this disorder are constantly seeking admiration and attention — they're more concerned with appearances than with substance — such as being seen with the *right* person. Their self-esteem is often fragile.

"O.J., as other narcissistic people, can show great rage when someone he wants to control hurts him in some manner because the *hurt* touches him in an area of his inner self which could have been scarred in some way at an earlier age."

She further added, "He may have borderline personality disorder. The essential feature here is an instability in a variety of areas, including interpersonal behavior, mood, and self-image. No single feature is invariably present. Relationships are often intense and unstable with marked shifts of attitude over a period of time. Often there is impulsive and unpredictable behavior, that is potentially physically damaging. There also can be marked shifts in moods — from normal to abnormal — intense anger or lack of control of anger. A person with this disorder may have an uncertainty about his/her identity — self-image. Such a person may have a problem with being alone, and often experiences chronic feelings of emptiness or boredom."

Charts are cast for events as well as people. The night of the double murders, Simpson's chart was heavily afflicted. The highly charged moon in an event chart often stirs and conjures up dark and hidden emotions. It was also triggering the negative aspects between his natal moon and Uranus, causing him to lose control and *go crazy*. This aspect shows a person in conflict with himself and the world around him. To make matters worse, Mercury went retrograde (backwards) that day at the degree of his progressed Mars, ruler of knives and violence!

If Shakespeare had written the drama, O.J. would have killed himself during the car chase, a noble end that would have kept the hero legend alive. If the victim had been his first wife, his childhood sweetheart, Marguerite Whitley, the case would probably have not attracted such obsessive attention from the public. The intermarriage of a black man, no matter how attractive, to a beautiful blond woman who gloried in her body and wore provocative clothing, offended many blacks and whites. And the end of the preliminary hearing left millions of viewers lost, bereft of their *fix* — the daily excitement, the headlines, the radio and television taking over the dial. But as I see it, his fate, as Shakespeare would have put it, "his fault lies not in himself but in his stars."

The jury will decide the verdict. More information will be argued and discussed. The trial may go on for a long time. Far-fetched as it sounds, when we compare O.J.'s chart to that of the United States, we find O.J.'s Uranus right on Mars in the U.S. chart, warning of trouble, due to misunderstanding and confusion. *Tension all around us!*

The fall of 1994, late October, early November, was a crucial turning point for O.J., extending to the end of the year. There will be another turning point later, more at the end of 1996, and more troubled years. What happens after that will be tremendously challenging. Mars and Pluto, the very same planets associated with violence in O.J.'s chart can mean a serious life-threatening health problem, such as cancer.

The trial began with the selection of jurors September 26 just past the full moon in Pisces, opposing the sun in Virgo with Mars (war) and Uranus (explosions) colliding. But how could there be compromise with warlike Mars and explosive Uranus involved? On October 18, everything was at a fever pitch — tension! Suddenly his son Jason, born April 20, 1970 (also Adolf Hitler's birthday), under a full moon in Libra with the sun in a *danger* degree of Aries opposed by the moon, comes into the picture between the full moon of October 18 and the solar eclipse of November 3, which hit Jason's chart and the murder chart. What does he know? And Kardashian? And Cowlings?

Jason was born under the full moon, creating a deep seated tension within himself, due to the emotional and psychological stress present during the early years of life. Jason is also at war with himself. Living in his father's shadow, he has the need to prove himself to himself and the world around him. He is trapped in this tragic situation. His chart indicates his involvement. The changing picture for Jason shows he will receive more attention from the public — *put on the spot* — after the new moon eclipsed the sun in November and spotlights a serious turn of events for him.

The planet Mars entered the sign Leo October 3, 1994 and will hover over the ascendant of O.J.'s chart until May 26, 1995 — except from December 11, 1994 to January 22, 1995 when Mars enters Virgo for about six weeks — where it will make trouble in both signs.

The pressure will be put on the two main attorneys — defense and prosecution. On April 29, 1995, there will be another eclipse that brings everything to a head. In June 1995, O.J.'s progressed Mars will trigger an aspect of violence in his chart — a point of climax! At least the big show will be over — as Mars, the planet of energy, finally leaves Leo, the sign of show business, after its remarkably long stay since the fall of 1994.

The planet Pluto was on the midheaven at the time of the murder, joined to the north node of the moon. This means Pluto was in control! And Pluto is associated with drugs! At O.J.'s birth, Pluto was in his "twelfth house" representing secrets and enemies. Drugs have played a leading role in this drama! Pluto is also the planet of mystery — mysteries which O.J. does not dare to divulge. By June 1995 he may be sentenced to prison or suffer some form of violence. All along, O.J.'s health will be under stress (or "deteriorating") both physically and mentally.

Assuming he lives, he may be retried. The case will probably drag on until the end of the century. No matter what the outcome, the case will be discussed and argued by the public for years to come as O.J. Simpson continues to deny his guilt and to maintain an attitude of aloofness, even indifference, to what he considers to be a lack of understanding on the part of those around him! O.J.'s pride will keep him going as he writes his story to hold center stage. *To lose it would truly be the end for O.J.!*

P.S.

What about the children? Everyone wants to know, and unfortunately there is not much I can say at the present, because I don't know the time of birth for either one. I hope to learn them soon.

Meanwhile, I can only comment on the dates of birth as given, and of course, this means only generalities which will apply to many others born on the same dates.

Adorable Sydney, born October 17, 1985, has the sun in Libra, on her mother's ascendant, sharing the charm and beauty of that sign. The moon was in idealistic and friendly Sagittarius. She will be surrounded by friends and will enjoy a loving relationship with her younger brother, Justin, and with the relatives who will bring her up. She has talents for dancing, acting, perhaps writing. She would make an inspirational teacher.

It looks to me as though she will survive this awful tragedy and learn to take a positive approach to life. Certainly the next seven years will be difficult, but she will feel her mother's love in everything she does. Nicole's progressed moon is right on Jupiter in Sydney's chart now, at this point in her life, bringing her a spiritual protection, a guiding light. This time the mother's death will bring beauty as well as tragedy, and Sydney may learn to control her tendency to fantasize and channel her fantasies into creativity.

As to her brother Justin, born August 6, 1988, in the Los Angeles area, he has the sun in Leo and the moon in Gemini! A very *different* personality — a natural for athletics and/or show business, like his dad. Also a strong personality like his father, with the dynamics of Leo — a touch of the dramatic, plus the strong ego which must dominate the situation! However, the moon in Gemini tells us there is a another side to the personality too — much fun, a great sense of humor, a raconteur (the stand-up comedian)! He's really like two people and can switch from one personality to the other, unexpectedly and suddenly. Very serious and even moody one moment, then light-hearted and amusing the next — *difficult* to understand!

His chart shows a whole new life starting now — *naturally*! Actually it is better for him, his own growth and development as a person, to be out from under his father's shadow. Like his sister, he'll go through severe trials in the next few years, especially during the next four or five years. Then his life will straighten out and quiet down. If I can learn his time of birth, an exact chart can be calculated and analyzed. In-depth counseling by an experienced, trained counselor should be used to guide him. Certainly his chart indicates there is some inside knowledge here which must come out — and it may already be discovered by the time you read this.

DEATH OF A GEMINI TYCOON
– NEPTUNE AT WORK!

Geminis are the most magical lovers in the world. I know — I was married to one — inventive, imaginative, never boring, always alert to nuances and opportunities. They can be enormous fun. But they can change in an instant, like quicksilver, and leave you with a broken heart — *or keep you laughing for the rest of your life!*

I was pinned against the wall of the fancy London apartment of a hostess I did not know, wishing I was a million miles away, home in Chicago. I'd been in Italy, Paris, and now I was renting a room in a Soho flat belonging to the sister of one of my clients. She had been kind, ever kind, because she knew I was a recent widow. On this last afternoon, she had insisted I go with her to a cocktail party at Albany, the great old building where, at one time or another, the most famous writers of the century had lived and worked.

It was a crush. Although the woman giving the party was an American, she was trying to forget it and greeted me and my mid-western accent with indifference bordering on hostility. Elsie, my landlady, settled me on a bench in a corner and went in search of food and drink, previously having found that the grander the party, the faster the liquor and food disappeared.

"There's a rumor some royals might show," she told me. "If so, nobody can leave until they do. So let me grab what I can and then we'll vanish."

I was ready to vanish forever, food or not. Elsie, however, had been so kind, I couldn't be rude. My expression, however, must have left no doubt about the way I was feeling, for a huge man suddenly swooped down on me, saying, "Why so sad? Is there anything I can do?"

He wasn't the typical upper class Englishman I had grown to recognize. His clothes were obviously expensive but rumpled, and worn carelessly. The gleam in his eye was mischievous and wicked. Without being asked, he settled himself beside me and took my hand. I wondered if he was making fun of me, or just a little tipsy.

I retrieved my hand, "I'm waiting for a friend, who is getting me a drink."

"So I will entertain you meanwhile. I love Americans. What is your home port?"

I couldn't help smiling. "Chicago."

"That's an Indian name, isn't it?"

"And we all live in tepees on the lake front."

"Delightful. You must miss it. Now, I have a plan. I'm flying to the south of France tomorrow to try to bake some of the London fog out of my one good lung. I can see that our famous English weather is getting you down, too, so come with me. I have a boat there with a full crew waiting, and we can sail under the sun and stars. I guarantee — you will feel much better."

"I have no idea who you are and you know nothing about me."

"My name is Robert Maxwell. I know you are beautiful and sad. You won't stay sad if you come with me. I promise."

"I'm going home tomorrow. My passage is booked."

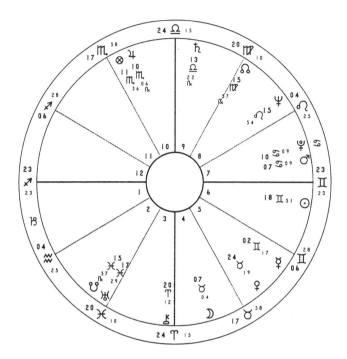

Robert Maxwell
Jun 10 1923   8:16 PM CET
Slavonice   Czechoslovakia
49N00   15E21
Jun 10 1923   19:16:00 GMT
Tropical   Placidus   True Node

"Forget it. I will fly you back home in my own plane after we've cheered you up. It's no good going back to that Chicago of yours in a foul mood."

I said, "And I suppose you own an airline, too?"

"No." He was suddenly serious. "But it is a jet and my pilot and I have crossed the Atlantic in it several times. Don't worry. You will be perfectly safe."

"I'm not so sure about that."

He was laughing again. "A woman without a

sense of humor is like a drink without alcohol. Whatever happens, I can promise you, you will not be sorry. I will call you later about details. I want you to come very much. I want to know you better. Seldom have I felt such an affinity to anyone as I have to you. Do you believe in fate?"

"In a way, of course. But, I have clients waiting for me at home."

"Are you a lawyer?"

"An astrologer."

He put both hands on my shoulders and turned me toward him. For an instant, there was electricity between us — the man-woman thing I hadn't felt in a long time. I was confused and more than a little embarrassed when Elsie came back with two glasses of wine and a plate of typically dried-out sandwiches.

Stiffly she said, "I didn't realize you knew Robert Maxwell."

"I don't. He came over and spoke to me out of the blue."

Maxwell stood up, bowed to her, and vanished. I said, "Who in hell is he that you reacted as though he was Count Dracula?"

"Worse than a dozen Draculas, in my opinion. Have nothing to do with him. I'm not kidding. He is a dangerous man."

"Dangerous? How?"

She didn't answer. "Drink your wine and let's get out of here. I wouldn't have brought you here if I had known — but of course he never can resist an invite when someone hints the royals might show. Do you know what his poor, long-suffering wife gives him at Christmas? A scrapbook filled with clippings about him and his activities, including those from his own scandal sheet."

"He has a wife?"

"One who looks the other way where his affairs

are concerned. Nobody can guess why she puts up with his antics. Maybe because they have nine children whom he does seem to care about, louse that he is."

"He wanted me to go to the south of France with him."

My friend stood up. "Let's get out of here. From the commotion, I figure the royals might be en route. We don't want to get trapped."

As we edged our way to the door, Robert Maxwell blocked our way. "I can't let this lovely woman out of my life. Where can I reach you?"

My friend took my arms and literally pushed me ahead of her. Maxwell called after her. "You can't escape me that easily, lady astrologer. Fate. Kismet. It's all there between us and you know it."

That evening, as I was packing, the telephone rang. My friend answered it, then came into my room. "Robert Maxwell is on the telephone. He insists on talking to you. I said you were busy. That man may act like a clown but I know from experience how dangerous and vicious he can be. I don't want to be in his black book, but I want to warn you. Don't have anything to do with him. He does terrible things to people, men and women. The saying goes that Robert Maxwell can charm the birds out of the trees and then he shoots them."

I picked up the telephone. That same damned electricity came across the air waves when he said, "I can't let you go this way. I have to see you again."

"You're a married man."

"That has nothing to do with you and me. You know you believe in fate. We are linked together and I'm not going to let you out of my life. Will you come with me tomorrow?"

"No, I can't. For many reasons."

"One of them, I hope, is that you feel about me

a little of what I feel about you and you're afraid."

"That's ridiculous."

"No, it isn't. I promise you, this isn't the end of our relationship."

After I hung up, I looked at Elsie. "What did Robert Maxwell ever do to you?"

She shook her head. "It's a long story. I worked for a publishing house as a reader. It was a fine old house, run by one of the finest men I have ever known. Robert Maxwell, on a whim, tried to buy it. My boss refused. He knew what he would do to it — cheapen it, sensationalize it, then throw it away, just as he does women. Then a few years later, when my boss needed money, he joined up with another publisher, only to find that Robert Maxwell was behind it. Maxwell fired my boss and everyone who worked for him. My boss killed himself."

I stared at her. She was still a pretty woman, although her blond hair was nearly white. Tears filled her eyes.

"You were in love with your boss?"

She didn't answer. She didn't need to. I put my arms around her. "But why are you still afraid of Maxwell?"

She smiled. "I wish I knew. But so long as he knows who I am and where I am, which he does, I don't trust him."

"Well, this is one bird he won't get a chance to shoot," I told her, "I'm off to America tomorrow and I'll never see or think about Robert Maxwell again."

Which wasn't, as Robert Maxwell had predicted, quite true. When you meet someone like him, the encounter leaves an impression. Even if you never see him again, you can't be unaware of his activities. Because of his restlessness, he was always in the public eye.

It seemed as though Robert Maxwell was haunting me. I was at a luncheon and one of the guests mentioned that she had seen Robert Maxwell in Naples. The next day, the *Chicago Tribune* mentioned that the British publisher Robert Maxwell was interested in buying the *New York Daily News*. About a week later, on my way to California to see clients, a strange man seated behind me was telling his companion that some crazy Englishman had paid a fortune for a little publishing company for which he had worked. But I didn't suspect that my friend Ingrid, a Swedish artist, would also make me think of him.

Ingrid had a beautiful oceanfront home in La Jolla, California, near San Diego. She is so generous with her home and hospitality, I wasn't surprised to hear she had a girlfriend, a Swedish journalist, staying with her.

"She has man trouble, " she told me. "In all the time I've known her, she could have any man she wanted. But she has been very choosey. Now some idiot has walked out on her at a time when she was sick, and it's been a bad blow. When I found out she was holed-up in some dismal hospital in London trying to shake a bad case of pneumonia, I insisted she come here. Now her health is better, but she still hasn't gotten over what he did to her. I think you might give her the perspective she badly needs. Would you do her chart?"

"I'd be glad to if she speaks English. My Swedish is non-existent."

"She's fluent in both English and French. In fact, she was working for a British newspaper in London."

So it was arranged that Kinska should come to my hotel. What I didn't expect was the long-legged glamorous blonde who, in a city inured to Hollywood stars, managed to turn heads when she entered the lobby. She had something seldom seen around these parts — real class. And her slightly accented English contributed to her charm. I couldn't imagine how any man in his right senses could resist her.

There are over seventeen hundred factors to be considered in any person's horoscope, so interpreting one is not simple. The sun sign — the sign the sun is in at the time of a person's birth — is important, as well as the sign the moon is in, the sign Venus, the planet of love, is in, and on through many planetary aspects all calculated for the precise moment of birth at the exact latitude and longitude of the birth place! That is why knowing the individual pattern can indicate the right and wrong times for making decisions.

Kinska had her sun in Virgo, whose ruling planet is Mercury, which signifies intellect and analytical reasoning. Her Venus, however, was joined with Neptune in the charming sign of Libra which explains her glamour and extraordinary beauty. And with a witty, playful, fun-loving Sagittarian moon on her ascendant, I could see what a formidable journalist she could become. Beneath the very feminine facade was a mind that clicked like a computer.

The man she wanted to know about was born June 10, 1923, in the Ruthenian village of Slatinske, then part of Czechoslovakia. That made him twice her age; another surprise. I couldn't imagine an older man rejecting this woman. She didn't know the hour of his birth — "I doubt if he does — he really has had an incredible life" — but Ingrid had wisely suggested she bring along some snapshots she had taken of him on his yacht.

"He must be very rich, to have a yacht, " I teased her. "Is he one of those middle European tycoons?"

She smiled back at me. "I guess he is rich, but

that doesn't interest me, as such. Most rich men are bloody bores. What attracted me was what he had accomplished, not only in Europe, but in Britain. Don't just judge him by his looks or by the way he is posing for me. We were playing games, having fun. He is brilliant. Please don't ask me his name. The things I am going to tell you are confidential."

"You mean he is married?"

"That, yes. And he is devoted to his wife who has given him nine wonderful children, some of them older than I. Our relationship had nothing to do with her or them. It was special — or at least I thought so. What did I do to turn him so terribly against me?"

With foreboding, I took the pictures from her. There was no question about it. The man I was looking at was Robert Maxwell — a bit less messy in sports clothes, but unmistakably the man I had met briefly in London.

"We don't have to play games," I told her. "I met Robert Maxwell not so long ago in London. And everything you tell me about him is just between you and me. Did many people know you were involved with him?"

She smiled that lovely, serene, yet seductive smile which must have made plenty of men her slaves. "He was a very secretive man. To me, keeping our affair — I hate to use that word because it was much more than that — private was part of the attraction. I met him in a strictly business situation. My boss, the chairman of the paper I worked for, had run against Maxwell when they were both trying to get into Parliament. He heard rumors that Maxwell was Jewish and challenged him. Maxwell flatly denied it. But my boss wasn't satisfied. Even after it was over, he was determined to get the truth out of him. So, he gave me the assignment of trying to find out.

"I called Maxwell; he suggested we meet at the grill restaurant in the Savoy Hotel, which is the place businessmen go to be seen at noon. I led up to the question with lots of trivia. I thought it would be fun to lead him on and then puncture the ego of such a flamboyant big shot. But, I could see him getting bored. So very sweetly I told him I had heard he changed his name and joined the Church of England because he was ashamed of being a Jew. That did it. He jumped to his feet screaming that he was a Jew and proud of it and if my damned Tory paper printed one word accusing him of trying to deny that, he would sue the publisher and me blind.

"Labor laws in England are so strict that I knew as well as he, that anyone who sues, wins. I also knew he already had a long list of law suits pending and one more would be just another big piece of raw meat on his dish. But I just sat there calmly waiting. I didn't scare. Suddenly he began talking."

Maxwell had been born at a time bad for all Jews in Czechoslovakia. His mother and four other members of his immediate family died in the gas chambers at Auschwitz. His father disappeared, probably shot either there or en route to the concentration camp. When the Nazis marched into Czechoslovakia, young Robert was selling anything he could find on the streets in order to live. He escaped and changed his name several times in the process.

" 'But I survived,' he told me, 'and those bastards who never endured what I did try to demean me. Let them try. I'll show every one of them who's the best man. And I will do it single-handed.' "

Kinska raised her eyes to mine. "The only men I've ever been attracted to are people with the kind of intellect and self-confidence I saw in the man opposite me. I told him I wasn't going to do a hatchet job on him and my editor could go to hell. Then in the middle of the restaurant with all London looking on, Robert Maxwell leaned down and kissed me.

"That was the sort of outrageous behavior people expected of him," Kinska said. "It was a ten-minute scandal. But I was enchanted. And when he asked me to spend the Easter weekend on his yacht, I accepted. I thought there would be other people, but we were alone. It was pure bliss. We played silly games, like children. The snapshots here show him having fun with me. The sex was unlike anything that has ever happened to me. And for him, as well, he said. He made me promise that this would continue. It did — for many months. Sometimes we didn't see each other for weeks. But when we met it was always wonderful, even when the sex wasn't as great as it had been in the beginning. After all, he was a frantically busy man, which took its toll, and he wasn't getting any younger. We always had marvelous times. For him to turn his back on me — please help me understand."

As I studied the pictures, I couldn't help observing that Robert Maxwell would have been a good actor, but of course acting wouldn't have held him. His chart was amazing and it was inevitable for Kinska to be fascinated. She had the south node of the moon on his Pluto, a sign of karma, and they both had twenty-three degrees of Sagittarius rising — twin souls. They would understand each other, sharing the same adventurous attitude and zest for life. His Mars was opposite hers, tantalizing, making for an in-and-out, off-and-on kind of playful game. Their love affair was fun, but not sustaining or ultimately fulfilling.

His sun was in Gemini and his dual nature made it possible and logical for him to be a devoted family man and still be a womanizer. Kinska's attitude toward this duplicity — her moon was on his ascendant — was more than acceptance, it was understanding. She lighted his path, shining deeply into the dark reaches of his soul, where all his bad memories lingered. She would be good for him, and he would bask in her light, but never would she be able to trust him.

His whole chart was one of the strangest I had ever seen. His sun in Gemini, squared by Uranus, shows the turmoil, the strange and unpredictable behavior, the complex burden of contradictory energies that marked his life. The moon opposing Jupiter tells of compulsive fantasizing, a self-deceptive ego, and the constant weaving of facts and lies. In addition, the mark of cruelty to others is indicated by the Mars-Pluto conjunction, squaring Saturn. In his heart of hearts, while all the while embracing life, dominating it with his cleverness and humor, he had contempt for those he charmed.

The man was such a mass of conflicting influences, he put me in mind of a volcano, always on the edge of eruption. He was not a man I would have chosen for any woman, least of all the lovely Kinska. And the final curse — he had the dramatic "finger of God," so-called, the double quincunx involving Saturn on the mid-heaven with Uranus representing danger to family members during his early life, with Venus squaring Saturn mid-point. The tragic beginning of his life, the feeling of always being an outsider rejected, would be repeated at the end of it. His power, the empire he had fought so hard to maintain, would crash around him.

I said, "He is a strange man, stranger than I suspected. In a way I feel sorry for him, but he glories in hurting the very people who trust him. People like you."

She would not look at me. "Never did I want, or

expect, him to be anything but a friend, a companion. I knew how much his wife and family meant to him. I even knew, in the back of my mind, that this wasn't going to last forever. I had hoped that no matter what happened, we would always be friends. That is why I was so hurt and astonished.

"It was Easter. I had had the flu and he, with his chronic lung problems, always suffered chest and breathing difficulty when he caught cold. We decided to go to the Mediterranean for a week and get out of rainy England. I had vacation days coming from my paper and he, of course, was always the law onto himself. The flight didn't do either of us any good, but the sun was shining and it was warm on my aching bones. The nights were soft and soothing.

"There hadn't been any sex — we were both too miserable. But the fourth night, over dinner, he told me he wanted to hold me, whether anything happened or not. I agreed. Just then, the telephone rang and he went into the lounge to answer it. I could hear him talking and making more phone calls. Obviously there was some crisis in London. I wasn't surprised. I sat out on deck for a while under the stars. Finally I went to bed.

"He never came. Next morning, the steward knocked on my door and told me that the plane would arrive around noon to take me back to London. I asked if Mr. Maxwell was coming, too, and he said no, that he expected a party from London and needed my stateroom."

Kinska hesitated, unable to go on. I put my hand over hers, "Dear one, he isn't worth all that hurt."

She shook her head, finally looking at me. "On the way back, I began to feel horrid. I went to the doctor in London and he told me I had pneumonia. He put me in the hospital but I only got worse. While I was there, I saw pictures in his paper of him on his yacht, entertaining an American movie star. One of the royal princesses was in the party. They were all laughing — I wanted to die. I even felt like it until Ingrid heard I was sick and insisted I come out here to recuperate."

"Are you going back to London?"

"I didn't want to go back. I was wondering if I should go to France when I had a telephone call from New York. It was Robert Maxwell, offering me a top job at a New York tabloid he was buying. The very idea made me furious. I screamed at him. Then he said, 'Kinska, don't let a little love affair we once had interfere with your career. The job I'm offering you is one any woman or man in the world would give his soul for. You can be one of the most important women in America. Don't say no right away. Think about it — think like a man, not a woman. Then give me an answer.' "

"And have you?"

She shook her head. "I know some people can forget and go on from there. In a way, I wish I could. But I can't forget."

"Kinska, he is a strange, tortured man. The chart shows odd and incomprehensible contradictions of his nature. He always has to have new conquests in everything — career, sex, social life — to reinforce his conviction that he is omnipotent. He had to be, to justify his existence. His appetites are voracious — for more and more sex, food, power. He epitomizes the era of greed and scorn for ethics. Yet he always remains the outsider. That is why the actress and the princess mattered more than you at the time. If you had stayed in England, he might have reached a point where he needed you again. But you are better off without him. He is due for a tragic ending. Jupiter in the tenth house retrograde in a negative aspect to Neptune in the eighth house.

That, in astrology, is ominous."

"If he were back being the person I knew, I could help him. I was the only one he talked to about his early days. He said I could comfort him when no one else could."

"I don't know whether you want me to tell you that you cannot trust this man." Even as I said that, I didn't know if she would listen to the advice she had said she wanted. When we parted, I gave her my home telephone number and asked her to keep it in case of emergency — the emergency I knew was sure to happen.

Back in Chicago, I was soon inundated with clients who were sick or in trouble — or both. One had broken her arm just after she had a miscarriage. Another was in the midst of an agonizing divorce and was having psychosomatic back trouble. And on a raw night, my last client had just left after I had spent an hour convincing him that life was not over when his wife left him for a lesbian lover. When he in his storm coat disappeared, I sat looking at the March rain slashing against the window and wondered if I could possibly get a cab to take me home. When the telephone rang, I almost let my answering service take the call, but I couldn't continue to let it ring. I had to answer in case somebody needed me badly.

I recognized Alicia's voice and regretted the impulse. Alicia is one of the most attractive, vital women I have ever known. I am very fond of her — many people are — but she constantly falls in and out of love. Somebody once told her bitterly that she threw her heart away as if it were a used tissue. She is either head-over-heels in love or moaning about her impossible situation and has to break things off. There is never anything trivial about any of her affairs. She is a Gemini, and once, impatient with her trials, I suggested that maybe she should become a nun. I didn't hear from her for weeks afterward, until one day she called for an appointment. When she arrived, she announced that she had found the perfect friend and lover and was going to marry him.

"All I will tell you about him is that he is from Boston, an Irishman with politics in his bones. Now please don't tell me what you or your planets think about the match."

I let that go and we discussed her career. She had moved to Chicago from Los Angeles and started her own publicity firm. And recently, she said, her business had improved, largely because of Noel's help. He was a lobbyist and had lots of connections. "We are friends and lovers — the sex is out of this world."

"I'll bet he is a Scorpio."

"What if he is?"

"Scorpio and Gemini mix like oil and water," I said with a grin. "In other words, they don't."

She picked up her coat, slung her bag over her shoulder and sailed out of my office only to turn at the door and say, "Damn you, Katie."

Since then I hadn't heard from her. I wasn't angry at her, just a little annoyed. Certainly, I wasn't going to put myself out for her. "I'm just leaving. Pour yourself a glass of wine and call me tomorrow."

She didn't give up; that's Alicia. "Please, this isn't for me. An old friend of mine from California — an ex-boss — just came into town. He's had the offer of a big job which he would love to take but he's not sure he should. He decided he wanted to talk it over with me. But you are the one who could really help him. And he has to call New York tomorrow to say yes or no."

"I'm tired, Alicia. I'll see him tomorrow morning when my mind is clearer."

"He needs to make up his mind tonight. And he is in a state about it. His mind says no way, it's impossible, but he's a Gemini like me and he loves the challenges and risks involved. Let me pick you up and the three of us will have a quiet dinner — some place nice and pricey. Money is no object where Rob is concerned."

"I'm in no shape or mood for dinner out. I certainly am not dressed for it. I want to take off my shoes and relax."

"Then we'll go to my place. I'll send Rob out to pick up some goodies at the gourmet food store and I'll light a fire and we'll have an early dinner. He doesn't want a full-fledged horoscope. He just wants a few words of wisdom from you. I've talked so much about you he wanted to meet you."

"Flattery will get you nowhere. I'm worn out."

"You'll never get a taxi on a night like this. I'll get my car and pick you up in five minutes."

The offer of transportation did it. I knew that she and Noel had bought a condo together, a high rise with a lake view. He spent so much time lobbying for clients in Washington that I didn't know if he would be home. When I got into the car, she announced that we would be only three, Noel wouldn't be back until the weekend — as usual.

"As usual?"

She didn't answer for a minute, then she laughed, "Rob told me to stop beating Noel, that I'm not housebroken when it comes to living with a man. Let's forget Noel and have a nice evening."

Alicia's apartment was warm and welcoming and she lighted the fireplace. I was too tired to dare take a drink but I appreciated a cup of tea. I was enjoying it when the doorbell rang and a tall blond man arrived, his raincoat streaming water and his arms loaded with bundles. In the confusion I could only guess that the two were, or had been, much more than friends. She towelled his hair and fixed him a drink without asking his preference. Then she turned on the stereo and disappeared into the kitchen.

I watched him move gracefully, on the balls of his feet, to the stereo where he turned it down. I remembered that my Gemini husband had been so light on his feet I seldom heard him come up behind me. Rob slid down in front of the fire and looked at me expectantly.

I said, "Alicia says you're a Gemini, like her."

"I was born May 24th in Los Angeles at 6:23, according to my mother. But I don't want to go into all that tonight. One of these days, yes. I just want to apologize for dragging you out on such short notice. The job I've been offered is in New York with a pretty flamboyant Britisher who is no saint to deal with, I've heard, but. . ."

"Robert Maxwell," I suggested.

"Alicia says you're great, but are you a mind-reader, too?"

"Far from it. I know he has just contracted to buy the *News* and he needs editors."

He laughed, a nice, warm, booming laugh. "He wanted to keep it mum. But there are no secrets around here tonight. I never met the man before, but he certainly can be very persuasive. I've been going crazy making up my mind, I'm near fifty and I suppose it's that old middle age crisis. Back home, I run a successful talent agency, but recently I've had the urge to get out and do something different, more creative, like writing. I think that this is because I'm at the stage in life when I want to leave something tangible. This job is creative — editing and writing. The main trouble is, if I take his offer, he wants me in New York right away. If I move fast, I won't have time to sell my agency or take care of my other commitments. I might lose everything I have worked hard to build. On the other hand, if I let this chance slip out of my hands, when will I get another?"

Just by studying his manner, I felt he must have his moon in Aries, aggressive and compelling in his business dealings. But, like all Geminis, this compulsive and impulsive energy is not consistent. He is happy and loves his job until, one day, he decides he wants change. That is Gemini, full of contradictions. He always has his antennas out, his nervous system alert to all the energy fields flying around. I could understand why he was tempted by the offer, even as his head argued against it.

I said, "If you want my best advice, it doesn't seem to me that this is the time for you to make such an abrupt move. If you wait a few months, something more suited to your talents will come along. That is all I can tell you without doing your chart."

He startled me by jumping up and giving a great whoop. The noise brought Alicia from the kitchen and he put his arms around her and they whirled around the room. She was tall, but he was taller, and they were a perfectly matched couple, in harmony with the music and each other. It was such typical Gemini rhythm, I enjoyed it as much as they did.

But Alicia remembered her promise of an early dinner, so we ate soon after that. Rob said only, when we were getting ready to go out in the storm, "I can't tell you how grateful I am to hear that my instincts were right. The offer seemed so exciting, challenging, I felt like a fool to think of turning him down. He was holding out such a dazzling future to me."

"Maxwell is a charmer," Alicia added.

"Did you know him?" I was surprised, but not astonished. Alicia got around, where men were concerned.

She shook her head at me. "I went to Washington with Noel for some big gala and danced with him. I thought we were getting along like mad until he began to tease me about wanting to work instead of staying at home and having Noel's kids. That old corny pitch put my teeth on edge. I dug a heel into his foot and left him in the middle of the floor. That didn't amuse him or Noel, who called me a bitch."

Alicia is a double Gemini. With another Gemini — like Rob or Robert Maxwell — she would be charming and flirtatious. She is part Pisces, with a contrasting and critical moon in Virgo, enabling her to switch from sensitive and delightful to cool and clinical, detached, almost cold. This is not the kind of behavior a Gemini like Maxwell expects or appreciates in women. It was no wonder she turned him off.

"But I didn't want to influence Rob one way or another, that's why I called you. Maxwell offered Rob the job with the earth and a couple of stars thrown in. I didn't trust my own judgment. But I'm glad he's not taking the job. Personally, it would have been fine to have him nearer to New York — I might even move there someday — but not with that monster."

They drove me home and I was in bed by ten. Where Rob would spend the night, I didn't ask. It was none of my business. That didn't stop my imagination, however.

Next morning when I reached my office, the telephone was ringing and it was Alicia, thanking me, saying that Rob had talked to New York last night and was on his way to Los Angeles. "Did you like him?"

"Very much, and I think he is deeply fond of you."

"That's old history. I worked for him right out of college. We worked well together. But he was married and would not get a divorce — he said he needed two women — so I quit and came here to Chicago. Since then, his wife has died. Now there is another woman in his life. She doesn't like me."

Quietly, I said, "After I met Rob, I did a little work on his chart. You both are in a period of transition. His Jupiter is on your Venus, squaring your Mars, and your Venus squares his Mars. This is an erotic, voluptuous, but literally explosive situation. You and Rob are made for each other. Maybe you will never marry — that might not work out, either, because you both need your freedom. He is a man who will always have a wandering eye. Whatever your future, it isn't in various meaningless flirtations or affairs. That would be a waste of your abilities.

"Some time late next autumn, there will be a change in both of your lives. You will get an offer of a job that will really turn your life around. I'm not sure that marriage is the answer for you. With your ability — your need — to nurture and care for others, friends and relatives will fulfill you. Animals love you. So do children. Working with them can provide the emotional involvement for your loving nature."

We said goodbye and she promised to keep in touch. I began to receive a series of postcards from places such as Hong Kong and Berlin. When I finally heard from her, Robert Maxwell was again the catalyst.

The call came very early on the morning of November 5, and it was, of course, long distance. The operator said she had been trying to find me.

I must have left home en route to my office when she was trying to reach me. Then I recognized Alicia's voice. "Where on earth are you?"

"San Diego."

"It must be the middle of the night out there."

"I've not been to bed. The night editor called Rob with the news that Robert Maxwell was missing off his boat in the Canary Islands and we thought you might be interested. Rob is down at the paper now trying to find out more."

I didn't tell her I had already heard the news. I just asked her what she was doing in San Diego.

"Rob has bought a newspaper here and I am going to manage his talent agency in Los Angeles. I'm down here finalizing the details. I always liked the agency and now I have it on my own, to do exactly what I want with it."

"Are you and Rob getting married?"

"Perish the thought. He's just bought a condo and his lady love is in New York buying furniture for it. He's not getting married and neither am I, although I thought about it a lot when I was bumming my way around the world. We'd kill each other if we felt tied together legally. This way, we can have the best of all worlds and always be friends."

I gave them both my blessing and hung up to consider the strange circumstances of Robert Maxwell's disappearance at sea.

My first news of Maxwell's disappearance had come from a middle-of-the-night call from Paris. I shook myself awake to hear a soft voice telling me, "I hate to do this to you, Miss de Jersey. But after all these months, I need your help. We've just heard that Robert Maxwell has disappeared at sea."

I said, "Is this Kinska?"

"I should have called you before. Yes, it's Kinska, and I'm here working on a French magazine. I'm upset, as you probably can guess. That's why I'm being so stupid."

"What happened?"

"Nobody knows anything except that he is missing from his yacht. The last time the crew heard from him was when he called the bridge to have the air conditioning turned down. That was about eleven at night. He was always chilly even in that climate — he was docked in the Canary Islands — and he was suffering from a cold. Then late the next morning, near noon, when he hadn't been heard from, they investigated and he was gone."

I was waking up fast. "Did he drown?"

"Nobody knows. He had enemies, a lot of them. Maybe someone was planted in the crew to murder him. Or, he could have fallen."

"Or, committed suicide?" I suggested.

"That, yes, but it doesn't seem likely. He talked to his son shortly after eleven o'clock and told him to send the jet down to the yacht tomorrow morning. He wanted to come back to London for some deal. There are rumors he was in a conspiracy with the son, what he said was for the record — all the phones on the yacht are bugged — and instead had a boat waiting for him to slip off to some foreign country to hide until the fuss about his finances blew over. You knew he was in trouble financially, didn't you?"

"I've heard rumors from time to time, yes. The general feeling around here was that no matter how bad it was, Robert Maxwell would be able somehow to fix it."

"This time he was in pretty deep," Kinska said. "You're right about the way most people thought about him, that he would somehow manage to survive. I just can't believe that Robert Maxwell would ever go so far as to kill himself. It just isn't his character."

"Do you know something you're not telling me?"

There was a long pause, then she laughed. "I am going to tell you something nobody else in the world knows. Already everybody is suspicious because he was on the yacht without anyone, totally alone, except for the crew. Usually he hated that, either had an entourage or had only one other person, usually a woman. They're hunting for some female who may have jumped ship or gone into hiding with him. I — I happen to have an exclusive on that angle but I'm not about to tell the world."

"You weren't with him?"

"No, thank God. But I might have been. Five days ago, on November 1st, he called me from New York. It was the first time I had heard from him since California. I left there because he was bothering me and went back to Sweden to visit my family. My father is a newspaper man and he helped me get this job in Paris. I don't know how Robert Maxwell found me, but he had his sources." She hesitated, so I prompted, "What did he want?"

"He wanted me to meet him in Madeira on November 3rd. He would send his jet for me, he said. I was so astonished I didn't hang up on him, which I swore I would do if he ever tried to reach me again. Then he said he needed me. He had never said that before. He was too proud to admit he needed anyone. I asked what was wrong and he answered, 'What makes you think anything is wrong? ' "

"Did he sound upset?"

"He had a cold — I could tell. Otherwise, he was just the same old Robert. I have my pride, too. I told him I had a job I liked and I was not about to risk it for anyone. Then he began to coax, but I told him there was no use trying. Later, from Madeira, he called again saying he was en route to Tenerife and asked, if nothing else, would I have dinner with him there the next evening, adding, 'Don't you owe me that, at least?'

"I replied that I owed him nothing and this time he hung up. Then this morning we got word he wasn't on board his yacht. The only thing his son knew was that Robert had told him to have the plane circle the ship before it landed. That doesn't sound like he was planning to kill himself, does it?"

I told her the Maxwell chart was in my office and I would be there by 8 a.m., my time. Quickly I got up and dressed on a chilly winter day, with the wind blowing with hurricane force across the lake. I had hardly stepped into my office when my private line rang. I expected Kinska, but to my surprise, it was Nicole, also giving me the news of Robert Maxwell. When I finished talking to her, I looked for Kinska's file, for I had put his chart with hers.

It was all much as I remembered, Jupiter in the tenth house which told of fame (and infamy), in negative aspect to Neptune in the eighth house, which tells of transition, sometimes through death. Neptune represents water, as well as alcohol and drugs. Here, Neptune suggests death by drowning, and in negative aspect. And Jupiter, the planet of money, was seriously afflicted by a trouble-aspect involved with Neptune, the planet of fantasy and dream-like aspirations. These ominous indications were in conflict with the moon in the sign of Taurus. The fixed T-square that throughout his life robbed him of fame, prestige, and friendships, had finally caught up with him. The complex man who fled from reality, who lied even to himself, who ran faster and faster, snatching up acquisitions recklessly, had finally escaped through the only possible exit for him — death.

When Kinska called again, I told her that I thought he had killed himself. She demurred, "It seems so out of character. Even his wife doesn't believe he would commit suicide. And he was talking with one of his sons that night. The son had planned to fly down to see him, but Robert told him no, to send the plane down empty to pick him up. His last words to him were, 'I'll see you tomorrow.' He always was so proud of being a survivor, of having strengths not given to other lesser, human beings. He was so much his old self when he talked to me, so sure that no matter what, no woman could resist his charms ."

"You said once you believed in past lives. So I suggest this. Saturn retrograde in his chart tells us that he came into this life avoiding self-awareness and self-honesty. He was determined, willy-nilly, to achieve the ultimate in power, control, respect of the world. If he had been honest with himself, which he never was, he would have faced the fact that he was beyond his depth long before this latest crisis. Perhaps that is what finally happened, in the dark of that last night. He knew he was finished. That is why I think he must have drowned himself."

"But why did he want me to meet him if he was going to kill himself?"

"It might have been all part of his plot, so you could confirm the fact he planned to go on living. I know he must have had heavy insurance, but in most cases, it is revoked if the person commits suicide. It was his last little hoax — as much to preserve his reputation in front of the world as to save the money for his wife and children."

"Somehow, it makes me sad to think of his ending that way, no more a survivor than the other Jews who died in the Nazi gas chambers. Devil that he was, I would rather think of him sitting on a desert island with his arm around some babe than feeding fishes. There already are rumors that some tart was aboard and he dared her to toss him into the briny.

The way he used to tease, she may have done so. Maybe if I had been in her shoes, I might have thrown him overboard."

"Kinska, one thing. Only you and I know you might have been there so put it out of your mind. There will be all sorts of rumors flying around."

"There already are, and every paper in France and England is on the story."

"And in America, I'm sure. I just had a call from San Diego and a paper there had the news on its wire service."

Then I added, "Remember, I told you you were lucky, he wasn't the man for you. The very crassness of his thinking that he could get you back when he whistled shows you the kind of man he was."

"I know. And thanks. I'll call you if I find out anything more." Tears choked her voice.

Next morning she called again, telling me that Robert Maxwell's body had been found that night near shore, and recovered. An autopsy was being done hurriedly because the family wanted to take him to Israel for burial. Their theory was that someone had been planted aboard the yacht to kill him.

"But you still think it was suicide?"

"It looks that way in the chart."

"Nobody else thinks so, especially the family. He didn't leave any notes. And the worst part — if he killed himself, the family won't get a dime. The last thing he told his son was to have the plane circle the yacht as usual, before it landed. He was insured for $35 million with Lloyd's of London but only in case of natural or accidental death. They say they are penniless now. It seems cruel that he didn't find some way of providing for them. The family says he just wouldn't do that to them."

"Unless he thought he could get away with still another fraud. He may have hoped to make his suicide appear to be an accident — the final fantasy gone wrong!"

The funeral services were held in the Mount of Olives, the world's largest Jewish cemetery, in Jerusalem. Over the coffin, a few kind words were said. He was praised for the many investments he had made in Israel, for the help he had given to Russian Jews trying to emigrate to Israel. But that was all. I read afterward that there were few mourners, except the family.

All the world seemed to turn against him. He was reviled in public and in private. The English royal family, which he had run after so flagrantly made fun of him, calling him "Cap'n Crook." Even his own paper joined in the abuse. Sycophants were the first to denounce him. All his dirty laundry was aired — it came out he had even looted the pension fund of his own paper of many millions of dollars to cover some of his debts. He had no game plan. Confronted by creditors, he promised, "You'll get your money" and stole from other holdings to supply it. The thefts weren't for personal gain, but just to keep his empire going. His fraud was not sophisticated, he was a desperate gambler, often pledging the same collateral to different companies.

When he died, he owed hundreds of millions of dollars — everything he owned — his yacht, his Gulfstream jet. Even the furnishings of his flat, including his fabulous wine cellar, were put up for sale at auction, to partially cover his massive debts. The orgy of recrimination went on and on. Nothing anybody could say was bad enough. Even the old tales of his denying his Jewish background were brought up again.

Kinska later told me that her story about him in the French publication was the only temperate evaluation. That night, after the funeral, when the latest issue had been put to bed, she had sat alone in her dark office, feeling sad about the waste of such a man, thinking that in spite of all his faults, Robert Maxwell had been larger than life.

And indeed he was.

TAURUS – OBSESSED BY LOVE

On November 5, 1992, Sol Wachtler, the Chief Justice of the New York Court of Appeals and a man often mentioned as the next Republican candidate for governor, was arrested by the FBI on charges of extortion and harassing a former mistress, Joy Silverman, writing obscene letters to her, and threatening to kidnap her daughter.

The news stunned New York. In the legal profession, Wachtler was admired for his brilliance and the clarity of his opinions. Politically, his star was even brighter. He was a vote-getter, with his articulate charm, his intelligence, his suave looks. He was regarded as the key to winning the state for the party and the best possible choice to defeat his former friend and the man who had appointed him to the court, the gubernatorial incumbent, Mario Cuomo. And even more importantly, in the world of politics where reputations are so easily shredded, he was for all practical purposes, *spotless.* He had been married to the same woman for forty years, and was the father of three happily married daughters and one son who was planning to follow his father in politics.

Among his associates, he seemed the last person in the world to be accused of anything bordering on the charges. He was far from a womanizer. Joan, his wife, had been his best girl since prep school days. In fact, in many ways, Sol was regarded as a bit of a puritan. He disapproved of careless obscenities, foul talk. He had been known to reproach an associate with, "Watch your language, sailor."

But, after all these years — a scandal. Worse than a scandal — a picture of a man so besotted with sexual frenzy that he turned into a monster. Even more humiliating, the victim, the woman he lost his head about, was the step-cousin of his own wife, the ward whose trust he managed. He had ruined himself as a lawyer and a man.

I happened to be in New York the weekend after he was arrested. I had come for fun with old friends. On Friday we saw the Matisse show, the theater afterward, two shows on Saturday, and ended with a matinee of *Crazy for You* on Sunday. My hostess, Darby, is a photographer who often works for the theater, and her husband, Tim, is a psychologist with whom I have worked on several cases, both his and mine. They were busy people so I was moving to the Lombardy Hotel on Monday, where I would spend a week seeing clients.

On the way out of the theater, Tim ran into a man who had been his roommate at Harvard, a tax lawyer who came from a family long connected with Republican politics. Tim insisted that Ira come back to the house and have soup and sandwiches with us. In the taxi, Tim explained that Ira was friendly with Wachtler and even before the arrest had told Tim that Wachtler wasn't acting like himself. He had tried to persuade the judge to consult Tim, but found out that Sol's wife, who was a social worker, had already sent him to doctors she knew.

Since Darby's housekeeper had the weekend off,

Sol Wachtler

Apr 29 1930   11:21 PM EST
new york   n y
41N00   74W00
Apr 30 1930   04:21:00 GMT
Tropical   Placidus   True Node

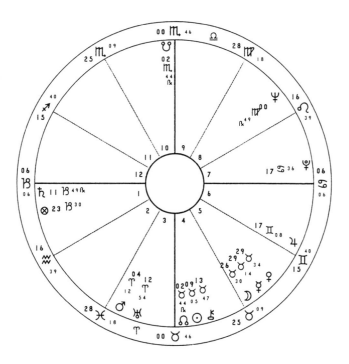

we all gathered in the kitchen. Tim heated soup while Darby and I made sandwiches and Ira set the table. Ira and I were on a first-name basis by that time.

Inevitably, the subject of Sol Wachtler came up because this was the first time Tim had talked to Ira since the judge had been arrested. Ira admitted he was deeply concerned about Wachtler. "I'd wanted him to see you, Tim. He wasn't himself. He was inattentive — very unlike him — and then would go off on long

Joy Silverman

Apr 8 1947   12:47 AM EST
Manhattan   New York
40N46   73W59
Apr 8 1947   05:47:00 GMT
Tropical   Placidus   True Node

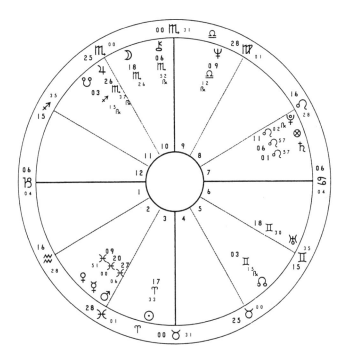

dissertations that had little to do with what we had been discussing. Not that he wasn't functioning at his job. But he wasn't himself."

"It's no wonder, when I saw all the pills the doctors were giving him, I wonder why he didn't go completely off his rocker. If he had been my client, I would have stopped them all and tried to get him to go away for a rest. Maybe that wasn't the answer either. I'm thinking he might be a multiple personality. Have you had any experience with that Katie?"

I said I thought there might be another reason. From what I heard, Sol Wachtler was a man so intent on working on his public image that he might have neglected his own sexual needs, suppressing them until they finally emerged and ruined him.

Tim nodded. "I've heard tell that although he and Joan went together for five years before they were married, they waited until the marriage to have sexual relations. It didn't make sense to me — these aren't Victorian days — but it might be that he was so busy making himself the top of the class, the best and the brightest, that when he finally got a taste of the real thing, he, as the kids say, *went ape.*"

"I've only heard bits and pieces of the story. Fill me in on what really happened."

The three of them started to talk at once. Then Darby took charge, "Let Ira tell it. He knows the whole story."

Ira was a nice man, I could feel instinctively, a kind man. It was obvious he was a little embarrassed. But I had asked a question, so he answered, protesting, "I'm no gossip. I know the harm it can do. But what happened here is obvious. The woman is twenty years younger than Sol. Her mother married Joan Wachtler's uncle when Joy was a little girl. Her own father had disappeared and her step-father had died; the kid clung to her mother, so much so, that old man Bibbs regarded her as a pest.

"You know more about that kind of thing than I do, Tim, but it was obvious the poor kid was afraid her mother would get away, too. It annoyed Bibbs enough so that he never adopted her, although he did her older brother. However, eventually, when her mother died of cancer and Bibbs remarried a woman whose name, Honey, might have given Joy pause. For, before he died he remade his will, leaving a large sum to both Joy and her brother. The catch was, he appointed Honey and Sol co-executors."

"Which meant that Honey would have control of Joy's inheritance?" The question came from Darby.

"Pretty much. Anyway, Joy went to Sol, a maiden in distress — not exactly a maiden — for she was on her third marriage. But she's a good-looking woman and a bit of a flirt, I hear, so she must have used her wiles on him. At any rate, he fixed it that he would become the sole executor and she would be his ward."

"And they were all supposed to live happily ever after," Darby supplied.

"But he fell in love with Joy. Went overboard. And after a while, she got tired of him. Maybe because he still had sense enough not to divorce his wife. Or, maybe she just got bored. After all, she had gone through three husbands. That doesn't exactly point to her stability, does it?"

"I guess things like stability don't matter when a man falls in love," Darby said. "Anyway, he certainly became besotted with her. When she finally told him she had found another man, someone younger than Sol, he just couldn't accept it.

"I don't suppose he knew what it was to be jealous of anybody until Joy told him she didn't want him around any longer. He couldn't stand it."

I asked, "What about this wife of forty years? Didn't she suspect anything?"

"I don't know when or if she realized he was having an affair. Maybe the fact that Sol and Joy were seen together at Republican functions seemed natural, with their mutual interest in politics. I don't know. Or, perhaps she suspected her husband was having an innocent flirtation and didn't want to make a fuss. After all, they had been married a long time.

"Only when he became so very strange did she

insist he see doctors. They filled him with all sorts of pills — tranquilizers and sleeping pills and pills to get him going. I wouldn't be surprised if he sometimes got them mixed up. Ironically, he was functioning well in his job, traveling and making speeches as normal. But all the while he was going through this ghastly charade — over a woman who couldn't hold a candle to his wife."

"Joan was the perfect political wife," Darby added. "I sometimes used to wonder if she ever thought of herself. She was a private person, and once said that if he were elected governor, she would stay in their house on Long Island, not move to Albany. But she certainly did everything to protect him. If there was any trouble with the kids — and there always is, as I know only too well — she took care of it. So, naturally they grew up thinking the sun rose and set on their father. They still do. This is going to be very hard on them."

"What if he had asked her for a divorce to marry Joy?"

Ira smiled. "I'm not a divorce lawyer. And I have seen enough divorces even in my own family to know what a rejected wife will do. But my hunch is that Joan is a sensible woman. She has a degree in social work and now that the children are grown, she works full time at an agency. I suspect, to avoid a mess that would have hurt him and the children, she would have agreed."

"But, then instead the girl got tired of him," I said.

Ira smiled. He was a nice man. "It always happens. To a young woman, an amorous old man can be a bore. And even if she tried to dispose of him gently — and I'm not sure she did — he couldn't stand it. So he began to do crazy things."

Darby mused, "Outrageous things. It was like the

script of a bad movie done by a rank amateur. He made up a character for himself, a horrible character who sent her obscene letters and tried to blackmail her. He even got some kind of a silly device you put on the telephone to change your voice and he pretended to be an Irishman with all sorts of cinema blarney. They said he even dirtied his nails when he handed notes to the doorman at her building. It was shameful and disgusting. He sent a nasty letter to Joy's fourteen-year old daughter with a condom in it. He built a whole character picture of a desperate man, dying of diabetes, who needed cash. He threatened to kidnap her daughter Jessica, unless she paid him $20,000."

"Was there any rationale for all this?"

"He claims now he did all these things so she would come back to him for help. But he became entangled in his own game. Perhaps he even enjoyed all the machinations. The whole thing makes me sick. I considered him one of the finest men I had ever known. To me, it is a personal tragedy. I keep thinking I should have done something to help him."

I broke the moment of silence that followed, "Can anybody tell me when he was born?"

Poor nice Ira looked bewildered until Tim explained that I was an astrologer and might find the clue to what had really happened to the man who had been the respected chief of New York's highest court and a potential U.S. Supreme Court nominee. "All the so-called experts disagree. Let's see what astrology can do."

Tim was smiling, but I knew he was serious. And suddenly, I knew I was, too — I had to know what had happened to make this man throw away everything he had worked for, all his life. And Darby and Tim knew it. Tim said, "I can find his birth date and where he was born easily. And we can get some good pictures of him, which I know always interests you." He looked at his wife inquiringly.

She nodded. "Even better, I think I might find some negatives in my files and print them up for you, Katie. Once, because our big family needed such a big house, Ira persuaded us to let him use it for a fund raising affair. Because I am apolitical, I hung a camera around my neck and started taking pictures so I wouldn't have to socialize. I don't think George and Barbara Bush were there. But Marilyn Quayle certainly was and I photographed her posed with Sol's girlfriend, Joy."

"Joy Silverman was really up there as a fund raiser," Tim explained. "She was married to a rich guy, Jeffrey Silverman, who was one of the big donors. And Joy had money of her own. She took to politics like a duck to water. And she made a name for herself."

"She was a beauty?" I asked.

"Like her mother, Jeanette," Ira said. "Bibbs Wosoloff was Jeanette's third husband. I never met her but I understand she was a real stunner. And like her mother, Joy has been married three times. Not exactly in Joan Wachtler's class, neither of them."

We broke up soon after that, but Tim promised to call me at the hotel when he had the information. The evening was the last leisurely time any of us would have for a while.

It wasn't until Friday that I got a message from Tim. I called back and he asked if I was free for dinner that night. I said, "Yes, but let me take you. I used to go to Elaine's before she became famous and I think she still remembers me."

"No. Darby made her famous lamb curry and she'll be hurt if you refuse. She has some blow-ups that will interest you and we both want to pick your brain."

I arrived bearing champagne so the dinner was festive and we didn't get around to Sol Wachtler until we were drinking coffee. Then, Tim said, "I have Sol's birth date. He was born April 29, 1930, in Brooklyn."

That meant his sun sign was in Taurus. But more interesting were the enlargements Darby had made. One was full-face, talking into a microphone, the other was an outdoor shot of him and his wife.

"I got these from a pal," Darby said. "The one of him and his wife was taken coming out of a voting booth."

I studied the close-up. It told me that he must have something in Capricorn, the sign of the goat, or a very strong Saturn. If you observe carefully, as I do almost instinctively, you will begin to recognize Capricorn eyes and chins in many entertainment figures. Johnny Carson has the sun in Scorpio and the moon in Capricorn. Judy Garland, Clark Gable, Lucille Ball, and Fred Astaire all had a Capricorn moon.

"The sign of Capricorn tells of ambition, the willingness to work, to climb, and the need for recognition. Sometimes Capricorns are not especially tall, for men, but extremely agile, like the goat. In this picture that Darby has blown up, of Sol and his wife, you can see he wasn't that much taller than she. But he was well built, so you wouldn't think of him as a small man. But most important — *Capricornians are relentless in the pursuit of their ambition*. They climb to the top of the hill, and if they slip back, they start the ascent all over again. While other creatures go off to frolic and gambol, the Capricorn stays put. Often the Capricorn-type doesn't even realize the depth of what drives him. He/she wants money, yes, but not for the things it buys — but for the power. And without realizing it, the Capricornian uses people. One has to, in politics."

When I summarized this for Tim, he said, "Sol was a great speech-maker. Lawyers are pretty much like actors, you know, and he really enjoyed the applause, the recognition. Sometimes it seemed to me he didn't need to give as many speeches as he did, but I'm a heretic, not a politician."

"I'm going to do his chart. Without the minute of birth, these pictures help a lot. But I'm already thinking that the sun sign in Taurus gives me another angle on this curious man. Taurus is the bull and Taureans are loving and affectionate and — above all — stubborn as bulls. They grow up demanding affection, either because in some way they feel rejected — or, on the other hand, were so adored and indulged as children, they grow up expecting more and more adulation as the years go on. They just can't get enough!"

"I would think the latter is true of Sol. I understand he was always brilliant and a leader. His father didn't have that much money, I heard, but even in the Depression he let Sol's brothers and sisters work in his jewelry shop, but not Sol. He had to go to a good prep school, a good college. And, to give Sol his due, he always lived up to that promise, and more. He was not a young man who wasted his opportunities. He always was the best."

"And then he ruins everything by falling in love with a girl totally unlike his wife."

"Many brilliant men make damn fools of themselves over women. But Sol didn't seem to be the type. And she certainly was an odd choice for a smart man. She was obviously a beauty. But also never serious — she had flirtations and affairs all her life, like her mother."

"Maybe it was delayed adolescence. Suddenly he

wants to hang on to his youth before it's too late."

"And then the object of all this late in life attraction decides she doesn't want him anymore. I don't know the woman but for my money, she is a bitch."

Darby stood up and went over to a cabinet. She came back with two glossy photographs in her hand. "Did I hear the word bitch? Here are the shots of Marilyn Quayle and Joy I was looking for."

She dropped them in my lap and I studied them, fascinated. "Here are two Capricorn-types." I gave one of the prints to Tim. "Notice the eyes of both of the women — round, goat eyes, drooping upper eyelid. And the chins, pointed like the beard on goats. These are ambitious ladies. Typical Capricorns will move always upward, never pushing people out of the way, but moving around them to attain the success they feel they deserve, the desired public eminence. And it often happens that the Capricorn woman on her way up uses men, or a man, as her stepping stone. Both of these women work that way, it seems to me. Marilyn has her husband. And Joy had Sol."

Tim nodded. "He coached her on how to get ahead in the party. And with her looks, and her money, it wasn't hard. I know some women resented her, but that is natural. However, Mrs. Bush liked her. And so did the President. They had her up on the dais with them often. And Sol helped her when she was suggested to be Ambassador to Barbados. Then, after she didn't get the job, she blamed Sol because he had coached her on what to say in the hearing."

"She must have been tiring of him even then."

"It was her inexperience and lack of background that was to blame. Not Sol."

Darby said, "Before you two tear Joy apart, I want to tell you something that happened the afternoon of the fundraiser. Ginny, our oldest, was home from college and I had her helping out, passing cheese and crackers. Apparently, Joy Silverman was interested in Ginny and asked her to sit down and talk. She told Ginny about her own little girl and how much having a daughter meant to her, now that her own mother was dead. Ginny told me later she was a real — nifty, I think she said — *lady*. And Ginny is no dope."

I said, "Capricornians value family. As Ira pointed out, Joy never had a father. Her own ran away, her first step-father died, and Bibbs rejected her. Sol might have been a substitute father for a while. But in her eyes, he failed her. I have no idea when she was born — I'd be interested to know — but there is Capricorn in her chart. And her affection for her mother and daughter are quite real. But, I fear the Capricorn woman is materialistic. Clothes and jewels mean a lot. Now that I have Sol's date of birth and your photographs I can work on his chart. I'm leaving tomorrow afternoon and I am off to California for Thanksgiving, but before I leave, I will have something for you. I promise."

And I did. It took some doing but at last we arranged a telephone conference call on the Sunday before Thanksgiving. They were expecting their children for the holiday so we were brief. Tim first had some news. After Sol was arrested, they had taken him to the psychiatric ward of the Long Island hospital where he had been a member of the board. There they kept him with his leg chained to the bed, watched by federal marshals. Finally, he was released to go home. But he had to wear an electronic bracelet which would report all his movements to the police. Despite the unpleasant publicity, his Court of Appeals colleagues did not demand his resignation. Wachtler himself took that step. However, Ira reported that he was in a bad way. He couldn't concentrate enough to read or go out even to visit his grandchildren, whom he adores.

"How is his wife reacting?"

"As you might expect. She is behind him all the way, and so are his children. His oldest daughter's husband is his lawyer, or one of several lawyers. Ira says the most stupid thing Sol did when he guessed he was being followed was to write a letter to the federal prosecutor saying that a criminal who had already been convicted, naming him, was responsible for the crime. Any kid in law school knows lying to the law is a crime."

"First of all, I think we discussed the fact that he is part Taurus. These last two years have been difficult for Taureans in general. The planetary aspects have caused them to do foolish and even crazy things, for Pluto has been in a tricky aspect, pulling the rug out from under them. Time after time, Pluto is the planet which troubles the hidden and often suppressed emotions. With my Taurean clients, I have tried to urge caution, knowing all the while I was dealing with inflexible people who are difficult to sway even when they come to me for help.

"Wachtler not only is a Taurean, with all that implies now, but he has his moon in Scorpio, the sex sign, and Capricorn rising. It is an unusual chart because it has a stellium____ a grouping of the sun, moon, Mercury, and Venus, plus the north node of the moon — all in the same sign of Taurus. This tells me that he is extremely fixed in his ideas, his opinions, his convictions and motives. He will never relinquish an idea or thought or method of operating. This very determination and carry-through which helped him win the respect — in the case of his family, deep devotion — of others, has also become an obsession. He is incapable of letting go once a project seizes him. To be denied his goal, or the possession of an object or person he thinks is rightfully his, is unacceptable. He will do anything to resist that insult to his idea of what is right. Any rejection, any block to this idea or plan, deserves the most extreme punishment he can imagine.

"So when Joy rejected him, in trying to ruin her, get revenge on her, he ruined himself. All those ridiculous things he did to hurt her brought on his own downfall. The way he disguised his voice in the anonymous phone calls gave him a sexual thrill. The voice is connected with sexual performance, witness the changing of the voice at puberty. And actually, I feel Sol Wachtler was at this time going through delayed adolescence in the sixty-third year of his life. He wanted to recapture his youth before it was too late."

Tim said, "It wasn't so much that Joan didn't love him enough — God knows she did and does — but that the adolescent boy in him wanted the same adoration from a younger mistress. Come to think of it, all his actions weren't those of a mature man. He was acting childish."

I laughed with appreciation. It is always good to work with Tim because his mind works so fast. "You are so right. That is exactly what I see in his chart. Pluto, the planet of hidden and suppressed desires, was opposing the interesting stellium of planets from the mysterious sign of Scorpio, almost literally tearing him apart. And at the same time, the two planets, Uranus and Neptune, which have been causing so much confusion and frustration in this world, were triggering another planetary aspect in his life which tells of rise and fall in public life — a terrific square involving Saturn, Mars, and Pluto — all exploding at once.

"Back in January of 1992, as he was beginning to play this strange little game, there was a solar eclipse in Capricorn which triggered the doom he set for himself. In June there was another, again in December. And in November, when the game was up, there were equally upsetting circumstances, plus a full moon in both October and November which brought the weird game to a climax."

Darby interrupted, "It was a game. I can't imagine a man of Sol's brilliance doing what he did. Maybe he was sick."

"Love-sick, obsessed with love. But all along he hated to hurt his family. Or the public, the people who admired him, wanted him to be governor. With Capricorn rising in his chart, he had a kind and caring nature and a quiet determination to live up to the expectations of others — his own father and mother, his siblings, his family and then all the people who admired and trusted him. He wanted to earn the trust and devotion bestowed upon him. He didn't want to hurt his family or his colleagues. It was just that all the elements converged on him."

Tim said, "Like the little boy who wanted to have his cake and eat it, too. But now Ira thinks he'll go to jail. The prosecutors are facing a hard choice. They hate to send a man who has been the most important legal power in New York to jail. On the other hand they can't give him favorable treatment because of his position. That would not be fair. So the situation is bad. The papers say that his lawyers are planning to use temporary insanity as the plea. Ira says that may help, depending upon the jury. On the other hand, Sol himself wrote articles knocking down the insanity plea and any good prosecuting attorney could use that against him."

"When will it go to trial?"

"Not until next year. Perhaps Spring (1993)."

"So it won't be a very happy holiday season for him and his family."

Darby broke in, "Sometimes I feel guilty with all our kids home and so much to be happy for, while those poor souls suffer. It can't be very good for Joy, either. I saw a newspaper story that said she feels like a prisoner of Park Avenue. She's afraid to leave her apartment, even now."

"You can't take the world on your shoulders, love," Tim said and we all wished each other a happy Thanksgiving.

The holidays passed and I was busy with my own schedule. But from time to time, Tim sent me clippings from the New York papers to fill me in on the Wachtler case.

On February 17, 1993, Sol Wachtler was arraigned in federal court. He was charged with five counts — one of extortion, three of writing anonymous letters and making threatening phone calls to Joy Silverman, sending improper letters to her daughter, of using his law clerk to compile files on David Samson, the man who was Joy Silverman's next lover, and one for lying to federal investigators. Joan Wachtler and all the children were with him and one of the daughters was crying. A note that Tim attached to the clipping said, "Ira says Joan kissed Sol before he went up to the stand. He looked dreadful, pale and thin."

Another clipping dated March 13 said that Joy Silverman's lawyers took Wachtler's lawyers to court to demand that she be designated as trustee of her own estate of 24 million dollars. Their documents showed that the day before he was arraigned he withdrew $36,655 from the trust as payment for legal work he had done in connection with it. But two judges declined to hear the case because of their past association with Wachtler. The case was postponed, with Wachtler insisting that if he were replaced he wanted his daughter, Lauren, to take charge of the fund.

On the second of April (1993), I had a call from Tim. "Wachtler is going to jail. The prosecution had hoped to put him in for eighteen months, his lawyers hoped for thirteen, but the judge settled for fifteen. The prosecution agreed to drop charges of extortion (he said he never took the money or planned to hurt the daughter) in exchange for his pleading guilty to charges of harassment. The judge also fined him $31,000 to pay for the security guards and tutors Joy had to hire for her daughter.

"Ira says it will be a few months. Meanwhile, there is the suit Joy has filed claiming her trust fund. And right now, although the judge relaxed the terms of his bail and said he can move around without the monitoring bracelet, he is still very depressed. He's on Lithium and Prozac. I suspect his doctors are still concerned he might kill himself."

"I don't think so. The Capricorn part of him won't permit that. He has dropped from the peak back to the ocean. But he'll pull himself together and try to climb back."

"It's a long haul."

"But his chart says he'll make it. Although going to jail is a humiliation, it may be less painful because he will be surrounded by men who have committed crimes, many worse than his. It could be better therapy than pills."

I had only one more clipping for my files. It noted that Joy had triumphed in her suit for the trust fund. She was to select an executor and Sol had to pay back the legal fees he had paid himself for 1992. Tim had added a note, "Sol goes to jail in Butner, North Carolina (later transferred to Rochester, Minnesota), right after the Jewish holidays in the fall. Joy must feel as though she's been let out of prison."

Sol's progressed moon in three degrees of Libra was opposing natal Mars. Prison!! A solar eclipse in Scorpio opposed his moon. I had been so intent on following the case, I was relieved to turn my concerns to other matters. And then, in the summer of 1994 I found myself caught up with another case — that of O.J. Simpson. Like millions of others I watched the famous chase. And, having to be in California in July, I also watched the preliminary hearings. Home again in August, I was amused, more than anything else, to hear that the TV show *Hard Copy* had selected Sol Wachtler to be one of their experts when the O.J. Simpson case went to trial.

Late in August, I had a call from Darby, with news that she and Tim were going to be in Chicago on Labor Day. "We're driving our youngest, Patrick, to Evanston. He's starting college at Northwestern and Tim thinks we may have to hire a truck for all of his gear. But we're staying in a hotel near you on Monday and hope to spend some time with you."

I said I would be delighted. "I have to stay home because clients from London are coming to see me, but I will be free from late afternoon on."

"That's great. I also have a bit of news. Wachtler, glowing with health, has been released to a half-way house in Brooklyn. He has to be there from 7 p.m. to 7 a.m., but he can come and go during the day and go home on weekends. His son met him at the airport and I was a good astrology student — I noticed in the newspaper picture that the boy had inherited Sol's Capricorn eyes."

I laughed and told her I was impressed. Then I asked, "How much longer must he serve?"

"Until October 28th. Meanwhile, he has a job — he is working at Sterling Equities, a company on Long Island owned by Fred Wilpon, who also owns the Mets. Wilpon's son is married to Wachtler's daughter Lauren. And by the way, I don't know whether you are interested or not, but Ira has Joy

Silverman's birth date. He was so cute when he called, proud of himself for remembering you wanted birth dates."

I did feel a stirring of interest. "Please tell. And does he have the place?"

"He isn't sure, but the date is April 8, 1947. If I send you a blow-up of that shot I made of Joy with Marilyn Quayle, would that help?"

"You want me to do her chart?"

"Not unless you want to. But I'm curious."

And so it was fate or kismet, but on the last Sunday in August, when it had turned so cold that I had cancelled a boat trip, I sat huddled over Joy Silverman's chart.

On Labor Day, I took Darby and Tim to dinner at Gordon and brought them back to my place afterward to show them what I had. "The first thing I want to tell you is that Joy was born the same year as O.J., but two months earlier. That means they were both afflicted by the same eclipse — and it was a *baddie*. When O.J. couldn't have the woman he wanted, he struck out with the only weapon he knew — force. O.J. beat Nicole and, in my opinion, killed her. Sol was in the same position. He used the weapons at his command — his fertile imagination, his love of play-acting. Joy is lucky that he wasn't the physical type. If he had been, he might have gone through with the kidnapping or even killed her."

Tim said, "The cases are similar because both men were so highly regarded."

"And the eclipse affected both the sex partners of Joy and Nicole Simpson in negative ways. There are very similar astrological factors tying the four together. When there is an eclipse on the day of birth or close to it, the person affected is unusual in some way — very talented with some hidden flaws or possessing some twists of character that blemish an otherwise charming personality.

"The eclipse also affects the other people involved in the lives of those afflicted. Nicole was the woman that O.J. couldn't have. The rejection syndrome was less extreme in Sol's case because of his own personality. Both he and Joy were self-centered and ambitious and conniving under the pleasant and charming facades seen by the public. The charm was genuine enough, in its way, diverting the attention from the less attractive person under the surface."

"They were more alike than they seemed, then?"

"Yes. When I finally figured out each chart and put them together I was astonished by the similarities. Joy's ascendant — the sign on the horizon when she was born — was Capricorn. So was Sol's, and in the same degree. This means a similar path in life and similar lessons for them both to learn. Does this sound too complicated?"

"I'd like to know more about Joy," Darby said. "I'm not sure I understand the connection."

"Joy has very strong planetary influences, combining the influence of three high-powered signs. Women with the sun in Aries are often willful, aggressive, even arrogant. As I studied her face in the photograph you took, I saw an almost perfect nose. I suspect she might have had a bit of cosmetic surgery, for the Aries nose tends to be longer, high-bridged or pointed.

"Aries women are strong and forceful. I keep thinking of the old movie stars like Betty Davis and Joan Crawford — both Aries. These were women who went after their men and got them. But after a while, they tired of the conquest and went on the prowl for someone else. While Joy uses men, her limitations mean she is incapable of receiving any man's love for long, or of returning it. The Capricorn part of her nature wants the trappings of a perfect family but her Aries sun could never manage it. Hence, her obsessive devotion to her daughter. Especially after she lost her mother.

"When I cast Joy's chart, I figured that she was born just after a full moon, giving her the beautiful luminous dark eyes. Venus in Pisces makes them appealing and feminine while her moon in Scorpio adds a subtle mysterious *come-hither* look, an aura of mystery. "Bedroom eyes!" But her Aries aggressiveness can spoil this charm. I'm sure that men often found her too demanding. She knows exactly what she is doing, except that she can overdo, overspend, overdress."

"That explains the divorces," said Tim.

"And sometimes the Scorpio moon may overdo the demanding sensuality, making her aggressive and arrogant. Underneath it all, she is quite impressionable. She tends to rely too much on the ideas and standards of what she considers desirable people — people in society, moneyed people, café society and jet-set types. Can you take a little more astrology to explain what happened between her and Wachtler?"

Darby looked up from the couch where she had settled full length. "I would love it. I'm eating this up."

"When I compare their two charts, the most significant factors I see are the planet Saturn and the north and south nodes of the moon. Karma! The south node of the moon represents disappointments brought upon one's self, usually inadvertently. So we can call this destiny, a problem we brought with us from a previous life.

"She has her Saturn at two degrees of Leo, blocking, literally squashing, his potential. His Uranus, the planet of electricity, joins her sun in Aries. This means he had an unsettling effect on her. One minute, he would stimulate her ability. The next, he would make her nervous and depressed. And she had the same effect on him.

"Sol has a curious chart. When I read that he had suffered a serious accident at about age five (which was suspected as the cause of a brain tumor, in connection with his strange behavior), I figured six degrees of Capricorn for the ascendant, indicating an eerie problem in relationships with people. It tells of an ambiguity in the personality, a strange shyness, even naïveté, combined with a certain craftiness and vindictiveness. Indeed, there is a tendency toward double-dealing.

"We see two distinctly contrasting personalities here — your idea of a multiple personality, Tim. One side is the kind, affectionate, giving nature of a highly involved Taurean — the other is the dark side of the troubling T-square formed by Uranus-Mars-Saturn-Pluto which uses people and discards them. But it is done very cleverly, so no one suspects. There is a clever wit here — so clever he could (and did) outwit himself. Meanwhile he enjoys his little games. There is a touch of genius here, or almost, until it alternates with the touch of cruelty which is waiting to cast a shadow on his insight and wisdom."

I sat back and took a sip of wine. "Is that enough?"

"More than enough. Fascinating. Now, putting on Ira's cap, I want to ask this — what is going to happen to him?"

"You know astrology doesn't predict."

"What do you think?"

"First, let me repeat, he will never give up. Darby said he looked hale and hearty in the picture taken when he arrived from jail and went to the half-way house. He will not give up. As I studied his chart, it occurred to me more than once that Sol might have been an actor or a playwright. Both Orson Welles and Shakespeare were Taureans. He loves playacting. I understand that when he was arrested and asked about his harassment, he took a kind of pleasure in re-enacting the character he had invented. Even working on *Hard Copy* would give him a taste of show business. And he taught creative writing when he was in prison. Somewhere, I think, there is a place for him. He can't be a lawyer but, as you said, Tim, lawyers are actors. Why not give it a chance?"

"What about Joy?"

"Her chart says she is cutting off the past. She went through a bad time. She was a real victim. When you look at what he did to her — during all the months when he was writing her threatening letters and committing criminal acts against her child — he was handling all her investments and paying her tax returns. In return for his services, he received a fee set by law. You can't blame her for thinking he was stealing her money or for suing to get it back.

"But that is over. And I think that the bad experience, like all other hurts and losses, had its good side. She won a battle with him in court. The lesson she learned must be to discriminate between the artificial and the real. She is forty-seven — a time when a woman is at the peak of her powers. She is beautiful, she obviously keeps herself in good physical condition. This is the changing point in her life, when she can leave behind the sham and emptiness and come into her own. Maybe this will be in the form of a man she can truly love.

"Maybe it will be a career — she dresses well and has an eye for fashion. I am reminded by an article I read recently about Glenn Close, the actress. She is forty-seven, like Joy, twice divorced and has a child. Her answer to her personal life and professional work is, 'You have to keep your arms open'. "

Darby raised her glass to mine, "Age doesn't matter. Maybe poor health does — but look at what some people with AIDS have accomplished."

"The answer is — it's never too late," I replied. "Which is what astrology is all about."

Update at Press Time: Wachtler has been released from the halfway house and will join the Legal Aid Society of Nassau County, New York, as an administrator in January, 1995. To date Joy Silverman has remained out of the limelight although much speculation from the public continues about her.

VILLAIN OR VICTIM?
THE ACTOR AND THE ACTRESS

In May 1990, Woody Allen finished the last of his editing of the film, *Alice*, went to lunch with Mia and the children, went home to stretch out on the big brass bed in his guest room, and then began the script of his next film, eventually called, *Husbands and Wives*.

Alice is the story of a woman married to a rich man. They are the utmost consumers. They have the best servants, the finest food, the most elegant wines. She lives the ultimate pampered life until she meets an alchemist who gives her life. What she wants is not her lover, not her philandering husband, but a return to the faith of her childhood and her desire to serve others. She takes her children and goes to work with the homeless, and becomes a kind of local Mother Teresa.

Mia stars in the film, but Woody does not appear. In fact, it is his tribute, his valentine to Mia, who had borne his first child Satchel, two years before. Satchel was Mia's fourth natural child. Mia came from a devout Catholic family and wanted first to be a nun, then a doctor. *Alice* was Woody's toast to the woman who, even as her career as an actress ascended under Woody's direction, has devoted her

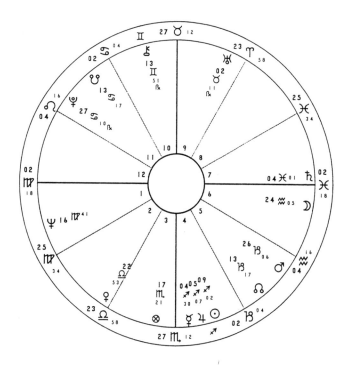

Woody Allen
Dec 1 1935   10:55 PM EST
Bronx   New York
40N51   73W54
Dec 2 1935   03:55:00 GMT
Tropical   Placidus   True Node

life to children — four of her own, and seven adopted orphans, one with cerebral palsy.

But he presents a far less saintly Mia in *Husbands and Wives*. It is the story of the dangerous age of marriage when some men around fifty-five or sixty (Allen was fifty-seven when the movie was released) are attracted to young girls. In it, Allen is a writer and a college professor married to a petulant Mia who is cooling toward sex. When their best friends announce they are divorcing, Woody and Mia are

Mia Farrow

Feb 9 1945   11:27 AM PWT
Los Angeles   California
34N03   118W15
Feb 9 1945   18:27:00 GMT
Tropical   Placidus   True Node

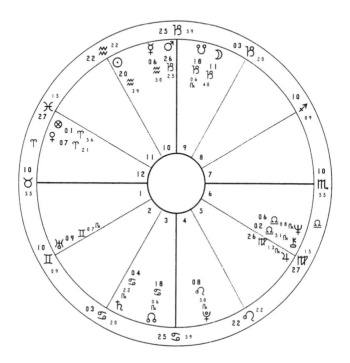

shocked. The male friend takes up with a young girl who *rejuvenates* him, encouraging him to jog and dance, and to generally making a fool of himself. Then a young student of Woody's character falls madly in love with him, admiring his writing and aspiring to write, too. He gives her the manuscript of his new book to read and she leaves it in a cab, a careless act which warns him off in time. He goes to her twenty-first birthday party, brings her a thoughtful gift, kisses her goodbye, and leaves. His friend also comes to his senses, discovering how boring and tiring youth is to an older man. A proper ending, and one with a moral. But it didn't happen that way in real life.

In real life, Woody was not as mature nor as smart as his alter ego on the screen. He made the mistake of looking at Soon-Yi, Mia's adopted daughter with Andre Previn, and finding the young woman desirable. Not only that — he left nude snapshots of her in his apartment which Mia found.

At the same time *Husband and Wives* was opening in theaters all over America, a different sort of drama was going on in court, a battle royal, a power struggle between Mia and Woody over the custody of Satchel, his natural child, and Mia's two adopted children whom he also had adopted legally. He wanted the children and she was a raging fury, determined to thwart him at every turn.

Astrologically, the explanation of this bitter hostility is simple. The planet Mars was on Mia's midheaven at birth in twenty-six degrees of Capricorn, and Woody's chart exactly mirrors hers in this respect. Mars, often called the god of war and sex, can be terribly destructive, but it also can be controlled, harnessed, and directed to make the person strong and remarkable once the hidden hostilities are brought to the surface and exorcised. In the case of Woody and Mia, the same energy that brought them together with a strong sexual pull was tearing them apart, and threatened to destroy the very children they battled over.

Who is to blame? As was all spelled out in graphic detail in court, Mia blamed Woody not only for taking up with her adopted daughter, but also for his "inappropriately intense" relation to the two young children, Dylan and Satchel. She first accused him of molesting both of them, but finally settled on Dylan. She made a videotape of Dylan telling in graphic detail what Allen had done to her. A team of psychiatrists examined the tape and cleared Woody, saying that the supposed harassment was the product of the child's fantasy.

In court, Allen testified, "I would never harass a child." But Mia refused to accept his statement or the testimony of the New Haven psychiatrists. To take a look at what drives Mia, let's look at her chart. She has her sun in Aquarius, her moon in Capricorn, and Taurus rising. She is family-oriented — hence all the children — but she has the stubborn Taurus rising. She will never give up when her mind is set. Woody has his moon in Aquarius, reflecting her sun, but since it is the reflection, she will always dominate the relationship. Certainly, she did that in the courtroom. Never looking at him, she sat calmly in her crisp little blouses and swinging skirts. While Woody, in his what seemed to be the same worn tweed jacket, sat looking for all the world like a man who wanted to curl up in a ball and disappear, which might have been a good idea.

Woody has his sun in Sagittarius. So did Mia's first husband, Frank Sinatra. It is questionable whether male Sagittarians should ever marry. Naturally restless, they resist belonging to anyone, yet think they need someone. This ambivalence leads to divorces and broken affairs. As Sagittarians constantly seek the ideal — which can never be found because it never existed — they are incapable of sustaining a long relationship. Both of Woody's previous two marriages failed. The fact that Woody's and Mia's relationship lasted as long as it did is probably attributable to the fact they had never lived together.

He had an apartment across the park from hers and she had a house in the country that he only visited, reluctantly, on brief occasions. Early on, he seldom, if ever, saw her children. He would pick her up around seven and they'd spend the evening together. Afterward, she went home and so did he. It was only later, when Mia adopted the orphan, Dylan, despite the complaint from Allen that she already had too many children, that he discovered fatherhood — and, to his downfall, fell in love with the idea.

Allen's rising sign is Virgo, one of the writers' signs. And his Aquarian moon was in the sixth house when he was born, which tells of his need to be alone, isolated. This is why they were both satisfied to live as they did. Aquarians have a certain impersonal attitude toward life, an ability to be part of the scene, yet detached emotionally. Woody's work is almost invariably autobiographical — he can put his own life in his pictures and often, impersonally, find a moral in it. He knew quite rationally that the affair with Soon-Yi was inappropriate, and his detached Aquarian moon made that clear in the movie. But in real life he made a foolish mistake which was to cost him dearly. The question I, as an astrologer, ask is, "Can he survive it? Can he learn from his mistakes in this, the second of life's crises and survive?"

Woody Allen has a strong sex drive, as he portrayed autobiographically in his movies. But he often comes out second best in his movies, losing the girl to some more prepossessing figure. Woody seldom wears make-up in his films and wears the same corduroy trousers and worn sports jackets. With his horn-rimmed glasses and his constant neuroses — the same he has in real life — he doesn't look like a winner, yet he has had romances with some of the most beautiful women in the world, on the screen and in real life.

Although he had been married in his twenties,

he soon decided that marriage was not for him. He said he didn't have time for children — anybody can have kids. He was innately aloof, and found displays of affection in public dismaying. He often said that the so-called affections of show business — the kissing, the hugging, the effusion of honeys and darlings — to be simply affectations. Many issues come into his movies as he explores the relations between men and women, but there is little explicit sex. You might not take a child to one of these movies because its content might bore him/her, but no modern child would be shocked by the sexual content.

Mia, although she surrounded herself with children, is incapable of loving anyone unselfishly. She was perfectly satisfied with the arrangement of living separate lives because she was not ready to accommodate his neurotic ways. She tried to fill the emotional void in her life with more and more children. But her Aquarian nature makes her incapable of loving unselfishly, even while her rising sign, Taurus, pushed her on toward increasing her family.

Interestingly enough, another woman who had her sun in Taurus, Audrey Hepburn, also surrounded herself with children. Both of these women were utterly sincere in pouring out their love for children, unaware they were filling a need buried deep in themselves. And both women had been deprived of their fathers' love at an early age. In Mia's case, when it came to a crisis, when she felt that both her lover and one of her children had betrayed her, she used three of the younger children in an attack against Woody. Even Woody had the courage to say to her, "I screwed up but don't take it out on the kids."

But Mia had to get her way — no matter what!

She cut Woody's head out of all the family pictures — while the kids looked on. They saw her send Woody a valentine family picture with skewers stabbing through the hearts of her children and a knife stuck in the middle of her heart. She encouraged Moses to write a letter, which was duly read in court, telling Woody, "You have done a horrible, ugly, stupid thing. I hope you get so humiliated you commit suicide. Mom is a great mother and finds the time and patience to play with all of us. All you did was spoil the little ones, Dylan and Satchel." She refused to let Allen see Dylan at all. When Satchel went to see his father, Mia told him to "wipe off" his kisses.

There is a reason behind Mia's need to punish Woody for making her feel left out. She was born February 5, 1945 with ten degrees of Taurus rising over the horizon at birth, which gives both the talent and need for self expression and public recognition seen in actors' charts. But this degree often brings sorrow, due to a certain emotional immaturity and need for self-discipline. It also warns of hurt and disappointment resulting from a childish tendency to feel rejected or left out. Her brother, Michael, died when she was thirteen, her father when she was seventeen. At nine, she had polio. And her mother was the talented and busy actress, Maureen O'Sullivan.

Add up sickness and losses through death and you have a woman who cannot get enough love — the old story — because she doesn't have enough to give. She never went to college, and married Frank Sinatra when she was twenty-one. That could not last. And she began her acting career in *Rosemary's Baby* in 1967. She was divorced the next year. Not long afterwards, she married Andre Previn. He was an Aries, a better match for her astrologically than either Woody or Sinatra. They had three boys and later adopted Lark and Daisy, Vietnamese orphans, and Soon-Yi, an orphaned Korean girl. Mia continued to act, mostly in romantic roles. After her divorce, when she was appearing on the stage in New York in *Romantic Comedy*, she met Allen and he invited her to his New Year's Eve party.

Allen, a wary host, met guests at the door and then managed to disappear. But Mia, impressed, sent him a thank-you note and a book, for which he had his secretary thank her, suggesting they lunch someday. They finally did — at Lutece — and so began the usual modern relationship which is supposed to avoid all the shackles and constraints that marriage puts on individuals.

Mia's chart shows that the greatest fulfillment in her life comes through her children. And Allen was so focused on his career he simply ignored children. He hated school and spent most of his time at the movies. He still dislikes sunlight, because it reminds him of the shattering experience of leaving the matinee dream world of fantasy and darkness and stepping out into the harsh sunlight of reality — just as a girl in *Purple Rose of Cairo* falls in love with the character on the screen but has to give up the dream because it can't translate into reality. Again Woody gives us a moral ending.

In his teens, Woody started sending jokes to newspaper columnists, and, by the time he was eighteen and a college drop-out, he began getting paid for jokes and sketches by comedians and show business personalities. Yet he was so unsure of himself, so terrified of life, he then began seeing a psychiatrist — and has never stopped.

He was married twice, once to an ambitious girl from Brooklyn who wanted him to become a great writer, as opposed to a great comedian, and then to Louise Lasser, who introduced him into the real world of show business. He was making good money writing sketches for celebrities such as Sid Caesar, but he knew that was not to be his ultimate goal. In order to move a step higher into show business, he forced himself to become a stand-up comic, performing his own material. Each night he went through torture before he went on, but he was a success. And, one night, appearing at The Blue Angel, which was the current hot spot in New York, a producer saw him and gave him the chance to do a movie, not only writing it but acting in it, too.

He was just twenty-eight, a significant astrological period in every chart because the position of Saturn, the planet of disappointment and sadness, indicates at birth that there is a lesson to be learned. In twenty-eight to thirty years, Saturn returns to the same position and marks a change, a challenge which asks, "What have you learned?"

And twenty-eight years later, in the middle fifties, the same cycle occurs as if to ask, "Have you matured yet?" The result is perhaps a reward for growing up, or a challenge to the maturing process. If you study this cycle in your own life, I think you'll be rewarded. It works in my case and I think it will in yours.

In Allen's case, at twenty-eight, he had reached the threshold of his life and career. He finally had matured enough to be where he had dreamed of — in the big time. His name was known. His picture was on the covers of magazines, he was in demand to write, to direct plays. Yet at heart he still was filled with self-doubt. He walked the streets with head down, afraid of being recognized. He would worry about his health, taking his temperature every two hours. All these neuroses are grist for his movie persona. But they are not so amusing in real life.

He refuses to go swimming because there are *things* in the water. Even when he was supposed to fall in the lake in *Midsummer's Sex Dream* — actually, his double did the stunt — he insisted on being doused with Poland water instead of the real article.

Mia was forty-eight in 1993, ten years younger than Woody. She is still in the latter part of her second life cycle, so the unpleasant court experience is just a turning point — the learning experience is ahead. It used to be that the approach of fifty was a feared period in a woman's life, but no longer. Women in their early fifties, like men of the same age, often reach the high point in their lives at this stage. I think this will be true for Mia. Her first cycle occurred when she was married to Previn and discovered the joys of motherhood. The second, I think, will be in her professional life.

Her relationship with Woody began to fall apart when Woody made the startling discovery that having children was a wonderful experience. He not only enjoyed fatherhood, he — being Woody — became fascinated by the new experience, *obsessed*. So long as her children were her exclusive property, Mia was satisfied. She even told reporters, "He has his career and I have my children," as though that explained why they lived happily alongside each other.

The change started quite innocently one night when they were watching a Knicks basketball game where Moses Malone was playing and Woody mentioned that Moses was a nice name. Mia had recently adopted a two-year old boy with cerebral palsy and named him Micha Amadeus. So she changed the boy's name to Moses. Although he adopted Moses at the same time he adopted Dylan, their relationship was never close. Woody played ball with Moses in the country but never for long because he didn't want to have to take a shower in Mia's house, "the drain was on the wrong side."

His real involvement with fatherhood came when Mia adopted a baby girl and — although he had argued against any more children — Woody became so emotionally entangled he wanted a child of his own. So Mia produced a son, Satchel. The two babies, Dylan and Satchel, became the focus of his life. Suddenly, Woody became a family man. Once, on a trip abroad, he found himself traveling with seven children. His closets were stuffed with children's toys. He would wake up in the morning and rush over to Mia's so he could pour the children's orange juice. On his infrequent visits to Mia's country place, he would creep up and lie in Dylan's bed, waiting for her to wake up.

His focus of interest had shifted from Mia to the children. But he, like many other fathers, left the details of child-rearing to Mia. He supported the children, yes. He read to them and lavished gifts on them — often forgetting to include Mia in his thoughtfulness. The bond between Mia and Woody was weakening. His sexual enthusiasm for her had cooled and when she discovered that he was having an affair with twenty-two year old Soon-Yi, Mia went after him with every weapon in her arsenal.

There is something that worries me in Mia's chart. It tells of a cruel, sarcastic turn of mind, a wit that can be twisted. The year 1993 was the worst of her life — it shows in her chart. She has said that she wishes she had never met Allen. But he improved her acting. Before Allen, she had only doe-like roles. He urged her into far more expansive parts. She is now almost fifty years old, and in the next few years, even before she reaches the end of her fifties, I can see her finding greater happiness, both professionally and privately. She may even impress us all with her achievements as a serious actor.

Mia won the custody fight, as was inevitable. In a scathing thirty-three page decision, the judge described Woody as "devious, hurtful and unreliable, insensitive, self-absorbed with no parenting skills." He did not, however, grant Mia's request to shut Woody out of the children's lives. The quarrel continues, she trying to revoke his adoption of her three youngest, and Woody talking about counter-suits.

The fact is — he has lost and Mia has won. In his chart, there are dark days ahead for the next few years. He has lessons to learn in this second cycle of his life. The main one — which Mia must face eventually — is that we cannot avoid our own loneliness by holding on to other people.

But he will survive. He has his talent and his aim in life, to be a more important maker of films, one like Ingmar Bergman. And he has his ability to shut out the world and concentrate on his work. That he has always done. On his sets, there is no joking or camaraderie. Meryl Streep, who played his ex-wife in *Manhattan* said afterward, "I don't think Woody even remembers me. I was on his set for three days and I didn't get to know Woody." Few people do.

But one who has observed him shrewdly, Louise Lasser, his second wife, once said, astutely, "The worst thing in the world could happen to Woody and he would go home, get in his big brass bed, and begin writing a script."

The real victims are the children. It may take years of painful counseling to undo the damage, if they can be saved. I don't know their birth dates, but I hope that someone wise and sympathetic will manage to salvage their lives. And I wish I could help by studying their charts.

Update At Press Time: In September 1994, Woody Allen was rebuffed in his attempt to overturn the 1993 child custody court ruling, when a higher New York court refused to throw out the 1993 ruling awarding Mia Farrow custody of their children Dylan, Moses, and Satchel. Earlier this year, Woody was forced to pay Mia's legal bills. Additionally, her latest work in *Widow's Peak* has been widely acclaimed. Further, Allen's new movie, *Bullets Over Broadway*, has garnered excellent reviews.

Allen has not been allowed to see their adopted children, Dylan and Moses, and is only permitted court-supervised visits with Satchel, the couple's natural son, for six hours a week. Allen vows to fight the latest ruling and continues to date Farrow's adopted twenty-four-year-old daughter, Soon Yi. Rumor has it that Mia has adopted another child since discarding Allen. Additionally, Farrow has decided to change Satchel's name to Seamus and Dylan's to Eliza. Woody has no say in the decision. And the squabble goes on — and on — and on!

THE GATE TO THE GARDEN OF DESIRE –
A VIOLENT DEATH

It is always with a sinking heart that I see troubled times ahead in any chart. Then I ask myself, what can I do to help? People cannot live without hope. But can I in some way warn them of danger ahead?

It is never easy — just as it is never easy for a medical man treating a patient who is terminally ill. We are here to heal and, when that seems impossible, what can we do? Many times, I've been asked if an accident or violence can be avoided if the person is forewarned. When a client asks me to indicate favorable aspects for surgery, a trip, or any kind of business deal, I can do that. But prevent a catastrophe which is indicated in the birth chart? I'm afraid not.

I can only tell you of my personal experience. I saw a crisis to come in my own chart. As far as I could determine, it would probably be an accident. Why didn't I avoid it as the time approached? For one thing, it isn't my nature to withdraw, to sit home, lock the doors and do nothing. I went about my usual life. I knew what was in my chart — danger. Yet destiny — fatalistic energy — was so powerful I could not control my desire to take a trip to Europe — but that's another story!

Afterward, in the wisdom of hindsight, I could

see specific information about longitude and latitude of the accident in my chart. But calculation is so complex, I missed it. Perhaps destiny made that happen. But even when we know that an earthquake is coming to a certain region, the calculation is so involved, it may be off by days, weeks, or even months. Which makes me humble in the face of destiny. However, when I do see real danger in a chart, what do I do?

Once when I was much younger and less experienced, a friend asked me to do the horoscope of her baby daughter. I saw violence ahead, many years ahead. Could I warn the mother of that lovely child and spoil her joy in seeing her daughter grow up? Of course not. I was afraid — I did the baby's chart up to the age of twenty. The mother suspected nothing. Yet she blamed me for not warning her of trouble ahead after her twenty-three year old daughter was killed in an accident. And if she had known in advance, what could she have done? Kept a girl of that age under lock and key? Of course not.

Now that I am older and more experienced, I do sometimes find ways of telling someone close to the client that there could be danger ahead and thus prepare them. But even in that case, I wait until the crisis is imminent and then tell that person. A doctor frequently uses this device if he thinks a patient isn't able to face the truth. In the case of astrologers, our dilemma is different because we can see tragedy coming in the birth chart. It is one thing to tell a very sick man or woman that it may be cancer because cancer can be treated and is not invariably fatal. It is quite another for me to tell a healthy, robust client that doom awaits, even if it is only a few years away. In every chart, the future is laid out at least in a general way. And today

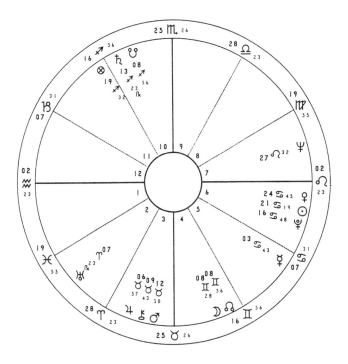

Bob Crane

Jul 13 1928	7:58 PM EST
Waterbury	Connecticut
41N33	73W03
Jul 14 1928	00:58:00 GMT
Tropical	Placidus True Node

psychologists and analysts work from exactly this premise — that you must go back to the beginning to find clues for future behavior.

Let me tell you about Bob Crane, whom you may remember as the star of the television series, *Hogan's Heroes*. The show was a favorite of mine, and even after it went off the air, I did my best to catch re-runs. When I was asked to appear on a TV talk show in Chicago, I was delighted to find that Bob Crane was a fellow guest. Sitting in what television producers like to call "the green room" after an old theater legend, I introduced myself and told him I had been one of his fans. He was delighted, and so was his pretty young wife. While he was being interviewed, Pat Crane told me she was his second wife and had been a model when she married him on October 16, 1970. They had been married five years. Then it was my turn on camera. I was surprised when I came off stage to find that they had waited for me and asked me to have dinner with them.

Soon we were on a first-name basis — show business is like that — and I found them both congenial and amusing. He had a lively sense of humor and told many amusing stories about his career. I was interested to notice that, although Pat Crane must have heard them before, she seemed to enjoy them as much as I did. Then he became serious and asked if I would do his horoscope.

"I've been depressed lately," he confessed. " I can't find a show I like, and I'm not even getting residuals from *Hogan's Heroes,* so I am just about broke. I would like to know what you think is ahead for me."

They were leaving for the Coast the next evening, so I told them I would see him around lunch time. But as I calculated his chart, I felt sick at heart at what I saw. There was no question that the attractive actor sitting opposite me was a ticking time bomb. And the explosion would take place when his ascendant reached the point of twenty-two to twenty-three degrees of Aries — the midpoint between Uranus and Mars — at the time of his birth, which he told me had been July 13, 1928 at 8 p.m. eastern standard time (actually 7:58 p.m. EST/8:58 p.m. EDT) — with Mars conjunct Uranus in the first house. There was a fixed star on July 14 and 15 — I already was aware of that because I had done the chart of a friend born July 14. This fixed star is one of extreme will power, strong conviction that no one can sway. Whatever the route this man went, no one could dissuade him.

The first "house" is the area of self expression, often important in the chart of an actor, for obvious reasons. And it would progress to the Mars-Uranus midpoint with Uranus ruling the progressed chart! The result would be sex, violence, sudden erratic behavior and probably, death. Looking at it, I wondered if it might mean suicide somehow connected with sex.

There are several hundred factors to be considered in the calculation and interpretation of a specific event. Every experienced astrologer has them stored in the computer of the brain, ready to pull them out. Of the 360 degrees in the circle of the zodiac, each has its special significance on the emotional and psychological level. Each planet, and the ascendant, occupies one of these degrees at the moment of birth and each has its own special significance in the psychological, emotional, and spiritual levels. As the individual goes through life, these degrees keep changing. The ascendant, or rising sign, moves one or two degrees every four minutes. That is why we often see the dramatic difference between identical twins born only a few minutes apart — because the ascendant has moved into another degree by the time the second twin comes out of the mother. So we have a different person!

The moon also moves faster than the sun, approximately one degree every two hours. Thus, the rising sign and the moon sign will give more individual interpretation than the sun sign, although most amateurs' seldom consider anything but the sun sign.

We find that multi-talented people like artists, writers, and especially actors have complex charts in which the ascendant and the moon are far more significant than the sun sign. Indeed, artistic people often are both complicated and unhappy. The British writer Henry Green once said, "Living can be a great muddle." Some resort to alcohol. Others become hermits. Temperament takes odd forms.

What I discovered in Bob Crane's case was fascinating. He was two people. Many of us are. A charming, considerate doctor often hires a *bitch* of a secretary, who really embodies the impatient, uncaring side of his nature. Or a gentle man may marry a woman who is a harridan, who does all the mean things he would like to — but doesn't dare. In Bob Crane's case, he was deeply split between a delightful, talented person and one who was indifferent to the point of cruelty.

He had his sun in Cancer and his rising sign was Aquarius, very different from Cancer, in fact quite the opposite. While Cancer is highly subjective, often somewhat touchy, yet always responsive to the needs of others, Aquarius is more detached, impersonal in its perspective on life and people in general. Often, the Aquarian will seem indifferent, unresponsive, even cold to more sensitive people. However, Aquarius does give an overview of the large picture that other signs don't have. Observers of the social scene — like Charles Dickens and James Michener — often have their sun in Aquarius, as do many other writers and playwrights.

Bob Crane's sun in Cancer, his sensitivity, made him the excellent actor that he was. But too often this sensitive caring man would suddenly turn cold, aloof. These shifts of mood were strengthened by his having his moon in Gemini. The Gemini sign produces a man with a highly sensitive nervous system, a quick mind and instant reaction to the constantly changing magnetic fields about us. This helped in his career, and like most actors, his career was his life. But his personality could change unpredictably and uncontrollably. He could become another person and a far less likeable one. Whether this had anything to do with his career, I did not know. I only know that his previous divorce indicated that he was not an easy person with which to live!

Wise is the person who is associated with a Gemini-type — be he husband or lover, partner, employer or child — if he or she remembers the fact that a Gemini is always changing. Forewarned, he/she can avoid being confused and frustrated, deeply hurt. And the Gemini also is often equally confused, wondering why others react as they do and often trying to blame his/her actions on others or on circumstances.

As I saw it, Pat Crane seemed to be aware of all these Gemini problems. She had stopped working when she married him, very unusual even in the seventies when working wives began to be the norm, rather than the exception. Either she really wasn't involved in her career as such, or she had the sensitivity to realize that an actor's ego would find a two-career marriage difficult to endure. Bob Crane was lucky to have found such a woman.

Even now, as a client, I could see him turning from a gracious charmer into a cold man, impatient with the details of what I was trying to explain about his chart. "The only thing I want to know is whether I'm going to find work. That's why I came to you in the first place."

I was able to tell him that there were favorable indications in his chart of a job offer which would be quite lucrative if he was willing to be patient and let the work attain its potential. "What do you mean by potential?"

"It is in a new field. And it has possibilities of doing more for your reputation than *Hogan's Heroes*. He whistled at that and left beaming with happiness at his bright future. And I was left with the problem of how I could somehow get in touch with his wife and discreetly warn her of impending trouble.

This was 1975 and Bob Crane was 46 years old. I could calculate that in about three years, his ascendant would have moved from the Capricorn-Aquarius cusp to twenty-two to twenty-three degrees of Aries, which in astrological parlance is the "Gate to the Garden of Desire." At the moment of his birth, this degree was occupied by the midpoint between Mars (planet of sex and violence) and Uranus (the planet of shocking surprise). And when his ascendant reached the "Gate to the Garden of Desire," his destruction was inevitable.

In any situation like this, I always ask myself: if I had detained him and tried to tell him that an unhappy end loomed ahead would he have changed? I doubt if he could have, even if he had believed me. No one has ever been able to avoid the inevitability of events that in astrologers' language" we bring with us." As someone wrote about the assassination of President Lincoln, "It had to happen and there is a kind of glorious pain in embracing that which cannot be avoided."

My problem of how to approach Pat Crane was solved when I had a phone call from her early in 1976. She informed me that Bob had had the chance to host a new talk show, be starred in it, but he had turned it down, because "I'm an actor, not a stand-up comic." Although later talk shows became popular (in fact Merv Griffin began his very successful show about that time), Bob's ego and lack of vision made him feel the offer was an insult.

Quite different from the attitude taken by Arthur

Treacher, English actor, of the old school, loved and respected by everybody, who played "second banana" to Merv Griffin, another Cancerian. A year before their TV show opened, I met Treacher as a client, and told him a whole new career would be opening up for him "one year from today." You've got to be pretty sure you're right when you promise something like that to a man in his seventies! And Treacher was so grateful to Merv Griffin for giving him the opportunity: "Ducky," he used to say to me over a Scotch at Sardi's, "This TV is unbelievable. All the kids all over the country know me now, and for the first time in my life I'm solvent!"

"I'm disappointed," Pat said, "We sold our house and now are renting a smaller one. I don't mind, but he is away so much doing regional theater, I am lonesome. And there is something else troubling me, I'm afraid that my husband has an 'addiction'."

I wasn't surprised but I waited for her to tell me about it. She hesitated and then blurted out that she knew about his problem when she married him, she realized that many people might not understand. But she and Bob had such a beautiful relationship that nothing he did bothered her.

Again she hesitated and I asked if she was sure she wanted me to know.

"I do. He told me he had a feeling that you were trying to tell him something about himself that he didn't want to hear. And I've been thinking and feel I should tell you that Bob's addiction is sex — pornography. Not with me — with other women."

Many artists have addictions. With Richard Burton, it was liquor. The writer J. B. Salinger became a hermit. And in Bob's case, there was an explanation, if not a rationale. At that time Hollywood was obsessed with "the new freedom." Young men and women — and some not so young — were adopting the credo that nakedness was an expression of freedom and promiscuous sex a statement of political seriousness. And a highly sexed man like Bob Crane might take this freedom as his right and not apologize for it.

"You really don't mind?" I asked her.

"He goes to these sex clubs and S & M parlors. The women mean nothing to him, and he would not ask me to join him in this kind of behavior, although it is necessary to him. We have a wonderful understanding and this hidden side of him does not blemish it."

I was astounded, not by her revelation of his "addiction" but by her acceptance of it. She was obviously an unusual woman and I had to know more about her. So I asked when she was born.

Her sun was in Virgo and she had her moon in Cancer with Libra rising. That meant this intelligent, sensitive woman had the sense of fairness and ability to see both sides of any point of view that Libra gives. I have my sun in Cancer and Libra rising, but I doubt if I could be so understanding.

She explained — in the course of a long distance phone conversation lasting over an hour and a half — that we must learn to accept other people as they are and not try to change them. I agreed with that premise, but I still felt she was remarkable.

Before we finished, she gave me the address of her new house and her telephone number and asked me please to call her when I was in Los Angeles. I promised I would, knowing that I must do what I could to warn her without frightening her too much.

Until I learned about his "addiction", I had been in the dark about the sex I saw in his chart. Now it became clear that the fate awaiting him would relate in some way to his fascination with so-called "kinky" sex.

After she hung up I got out Bob Crane's chart and estimated how long it would be before his ascendant would move into twenty-two to twenty-three degrees of Aries, midpoint between Mars and Uranus. It would be in late June of next year. So when I went to California in January to see clients, I would take that opportunity to warn her.

When I called the number he had given me, Bob Crane answered. When he found out it was I, he insisted I come to dinner — not exactly what I had planned but I could not refuse as I had to get in touch with Pat. The new house was small, but very attractive and the dinner excellent. But the rapport which I had felt between them no longer was evident. As I was leaving and he went to get the car to drive me home, I managed to have a word with her. She told me that she would call me at my hotel, she had something she wanted to tell me.

On the way home, the facade he had been trying to maintain dropped off and I could see how depressed he was. The work he was doing just wasn't fulfilling. "It isn't so much the money, it's the prestige I miss, the importance which comes with people recognizing your talents. You can't take the human being from the actor. I am essentially an actor. Nothing else really matters. What I do is a job, but acting is my life, the only life worth living."

Strangely, I felt as though he was in a way prepared for what was going to happen. But he was still not ready to hear it. When Pat Crane called, I was not surprised to learn she was considering divorce. "I've found out that he takes his son — the older son from his other marriage — to these sex clubs with him. And that understanding we had, it's not there anymore. The good years are over and I just can't go on any longer."

I said, "Pat, when I get home, I am going to write

you a letter about what I see ahead for him in his chart. It isn't good, so be prepared."

I drafted the letter in my mind on the way home in the plane. Then I sat down and wrote a careful letter.

"*Dear Pat:*

"*I am so sorry to hear of your decision to divorce Bob, although of course I am hardly surprised. Your chart shows that your situation has become intolerable. Your progressed moon, the timer on the chart, is now opposing your Pluto, the planet which brings conditions to a head — everything finally erupting as you are. You have your natal moon in Cancer which makes you tenacious and unwilling to give up. You persevere in a bad situation until — abruptly — you see the futility of it all and let go.*

"*Your marriage will end in June 1978. The chart for your wedding on October 16, 1970, warned of such a break, and Bob's chart shows violence catching up with him. There is an eclipse in April 1978 warning of a secret obsession-addiction about to explode — to come out in the open. Both jealously and vengeance are involved.*

"*Bob's ascendant (which describes the eventual significance of life's path) is two and one half degrees of Aquarius, indicating his inability to 'follow rules' because his independence is carried to the extreme of rebellion against things as they are and a disregard of all consequences for the sake of 'immediate liberation of the spirit.' So defiance is the result. The irony — and pity — of it is that if he could seek counseling before it is too late and learn about himself, he would find a greater depth of character and a chance for a real self fulfillment.*

"*However, it is over for you two. The end is in sight, and in late June of 1978 the violence I saw in his chart at birth will catch up with him unexpectedly. Many threatening aspects will group together in his chart, your chart, and in your wedding chart.*"

I ended with a few words of sympathy and encouragement. And when she received it, she called me. "I didn't tell Bob what you said about danger coming, but I did say that you suggested he seek counseling about his addiction. He was furious and told me he had lost all faith in astrology, the big job you told him about had never come through and he was through paying any attention to what you said. So I gave up trying to talk to him and am going ahead with my divorce."

And so it happened. In the early morning hours of July 29, Bob Crane was murdered in an apartment in Scottsdale, Arizona, where he had been appearing in a play. He had been savagely beaten, his skull crushed and an electrical chord tied around his neck. Nothing was missing and he was apparently asleep when he was attacked. The only clue was that he had been seen with an older man, a stranger, and that they had been arguing violently.

Several weeks afterward, I was in California and called Pat Crane. She asked me to come and see her. She was still in the same house. She went to a bureau in the living room and pulled out the note I had written her.

"It happened just as you said."

P.S.

John Henry Carpenter, the man who allegedly killed Bob Crane, was not arrested until fourteen years later and had to face trial for another crime before he could be tried for murdering Crane. On October 31, 1994, he was acquitted of the murder by the jury, due to insufficient evidence. I did not have Carpenter's birth date or time of birth so I could not calculate his chart; however, I do not think he committed the murder.

I am only sure the murder was in some way connected with pornographic sex. To me, the irony of Bob's having refused the job offer I had told him would come, because his fixed star made him too stubborn to accept the talk show offer, is that later in the year I read that the show he had refused was number one in all the ratings. If he had been wise enough to seize that chance, he might at least have died richer and in the prime of his career.

Incidently, I understand that a different time of birth has been mentioned for Bob Crane. However, I used the time of birth he gave me, *and it works.*

HOROSCOPE OF A DISASTER

Astrology is not limited to the interpretation of people and their lives. It can be applied to businesses, restaurants, and even buildings. A chart will give clues to its personality, its problems, just as it does for a human being.

Of course, a building is not a human being. But it is alive in its own way, created by the spirit, the genius, and sometimes, unhappily, the ruthlessness of those involved. Thus, it has its own personality.

I learned this lesson the hard way. When a beautiful new high-rise in Chicago went up, I was so enthralled by its design, created by a talented and famous architect, that I failed to calculate its chart before I signed the lease. With its view and balconies overlooking the river, it was breathtaking. My architect brother was enthralled — as he entered my apartment, he said he seemed to be already outside, as it opened onto my balcony with the river and bridge below.

By that time, I had acquired a good reputation in my field and the building owners were delighted to have me as one of the early tenants. Happy with my new apartment, I offered to do an astrological chart of the building. My heart sank when I saw it. The chart was terrible, describing the fiasco. Although the design was marvelous, the materials which had gone into the construction were shoddy.

Corners were cut in every possible way. And as the structure aged, and the maintenance was done in the same, cost-cutting way, the place became a mess, and the spectacular creation was ruined by the owners' venality. I stayed for six years because of the view, not the management. And when I read that the John Hancock Building was going to be built, I planned my move the right way. I not only did its chart for the moment it was finished — called the "topping off" — I made sure that the date I signed the lease and the time I moved in were astrologically favorable. So, as the saying goes, I have lived here happily ever after.

For a time, the Hancock Building had its own share of fame and glory. It was the tallest building in the world with all the attendant publicity and prestige. But that status was changed when, in the building frenzy that followed, New York's 110-foot World Trade Center, with its twin towers, went up. The panoramic view from the upper floors was majestic by day and spectacular at night, with the lights of the city creating a stunning panorama. At its top was the quickly famous restaurant, Windows On The World, which became so popular diners had to make reservations weeks, sometimes months, in advance.

Tenants came from all over the world, especially from rich Asian countries. A World Trade address was a plum, a mark of prestige. Tenants lined up as eagerly as did the crowds at Windows Of The World. The World Trade building claimed to be the center of world commerce and to be a tenant there was a badge of success.

But the beautiful building had a hidden weakness, what I would diagnose as a dormant illness in a

World Trade Topping Off

Nov 04 1972   8:00 PM EST
Manhattan   New York
40N46   73W59
Nov 5 1972   01:00:00 GMT
Tropical   Placidus   True Node

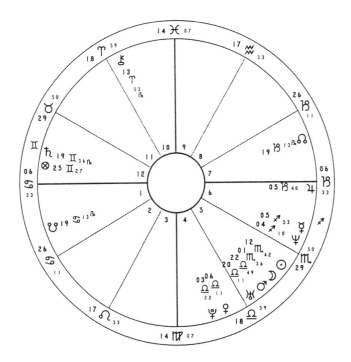

person, perhaps a virus. This became evident after the terrorist bomb exploded on February 26, 1993, wreaking havoc. Six people were killed and thousands injured in the harrowing hours afterwards. The electricity was knocked out. Elevators halted between floors, leaving frightened occupants huddled in the smoky dark, gasping for air. A group of school children were among the trapped.

A building engineer happened to be in one of the elevators that was halted between floors. After jimmying the door open, he and the group with him found themselves facing a blank wall. Smoke was seeping into the elevator and they were fearful of suffocation. The engineer remembered that the walls were made of gypsum and not concrete. Using keys, paper clips, and nail cutters, the group spent several hours chiseling through two walls until they finally cut a hole large enough for them to crawl through. They groped around until they discovered they were in a washroom. They found the door and were able to locate a stairwell and climb down 58 flights, stopping to help others who were having difficulty making the descent.

The bomb exploded in the basement garage, leaving a huge crater about 125-feet in diameter in which victims were trapped. Although many were hurt, it was a miracle that only six people were killed. But the trauma of those terrible hours left psychic scars, not only on the injured and those in shock from struggling down long flights of smoke-filled stairs in total darkness, but also on frantic families waiting for news.

Using the date the building was finished — "born" — and the time of the explosion, I calculated a chart which was revealing. The Center has the sun in Scorpio, a fitting sign for a building of such magnitude that cynical reporters called it, "Governor Nelson Rockefeller's edifice symbolic of tenacity and endurance, the survivor." Scorpio is the sign of extremes — and the World Trade Center was certainly that when it was erected. The impact of both the sun and moon in Scorpio emphasizes the independence, the pride in majesty, the self-centered arrogance that marked the attitude of those in charge. The World Trade Center was the best and, as the old slogan goes, "might makes right." For example, a client once told me that her Scorpio ex-fiance said to her, "You are smart, but I am a genius."

Scorpio also suggests mystery, something hidden. Moreover, the time of the opening concurred with "the dark of the moon," just before the moon joins the sun. The union is not strong yet and so the energy has not fully developed. This is a scientific and astronomical fact as well as an astrological one. The flaw was revealed later when it came out that the basement garage, which was accessible to the public, had never been bomb-proofed.

There were reasons for this. When the building was being built, the strength of the frame was not calculated with bombs in mind. The largest challenge was the wind, a vital factor in all tall buildings and particularly in the tallest ever built. Indeed, the only precaution was that the structure must be strong enough to withstand the force of being struck by an airplane if that should ever happen. The essential strength of the structure did mitigate the effects of the bomb, although that was a fortunate side effect. But there were also other hidden factors which made the twin towers vulnerable.

It was autonomous — not under jurisdiction of the city or state. So it was that when, in 1986, consultants told the Port Authority that the below-ground parking made the building vulnerable to terrorism, nothing was done — even though a six-story parking garage at Kennedy Airport completed in 1991 had been bomb-proofed. Later it also came to light that the building was arrogantly managed. Scorpio!

Indeed. For all the seventies and most of the eighties, the Trade World Center was the only first-class space downtown had to offer. Rents, which could go as high as $55 a square foot for high floors, were non-negotiable. Leases were inflexible. Service was poor, tenants would wait a week or so before a burned-out light bulb was replaced — and then the charge could be as much as $25. Cleaning was haphazard and it took weeks for the engineering department to okay a simple office change, such as a moved wall. With this attitude, it was no wonder that the consultants' suggestion to bomb-proof the building was ignored.

So we have this virus, this hidden weakness that was waiting to be triggered. And to an astrologer, the signs are all there — many of them standing out like neon!

The progressed ascendant for the "topping-off" chart was squaring Mars (serious trouble, calamity!) while the progressed tenth house cusp (reputation) was squaring the natal ascendant (more trouble). The moon at "birth" was joined to Uranus-Neptune in the explosion chart, and Saturn in the former was afflicted by the south node at the moment the topping-off was completed.

The whole tragic story is right here, for anyone who can read it — and for those who can't, don't you wish you could?

My clients have come to realize that in every life there is a lesson to be learned. And it so happened that the World Trade Center had its own lesson to learn. Its rising sign, Cancer, is sometimes slow to mature, often being too sheltered and spoiled in the beginning. And then something happens around the twenty-first year to make Cancers wake up to reality. They grow up, all of a sudden. And that is what happened to the World Trade Center. Now management is more aware of reality, the needs of tenants and the rights of city and state regulators. As a result, the building is now 92% occupied — this at a time when many office buildings are vacant. It took a bomb to do it, but the "World" has learned its lesson — at that tragic moment, 12:18 p.m., February 26, 1993.

Editor's Update: the four defendants, Mohammad Salameh, Nidal Ayyad, Mahmud Abouhalima, and Ahmad Ajay, all Islamic militants, charged with bombing the World Trade Center were convicted of all charges by a federal jury (8 women and 4 men) in March 1994. In its case against the four, the prosecution had traced the conspiracy back to April 1992. During the lengthy and rambling summation by the defendants' lawyers, the judge fell into a deep sleep and had to be nudged awake by a court clerk. After the verdict was announced, supporters of the terrorists attending the trial vocally denounced the results with vehement obscenities.

In late May (1994), the convicted terrorists were *each* sentenced to 240 years in prison, terms to be served consecutively, virtually ensuring that *each* will remain in prison for life. While appeals have been filed by defense attorneys, the convicted terrorists remain in jail.

At press time, radical Islamic leader, Sheik Omar Abdel Rahman and fourteen followers were awaiting trial on a related matter, plotting to blow up the United Nations building and other targets in New York City. Were they involved in the World Trade Center bombing? The U.S. government hopes to answer questions that were not answered in the March (1994) verdict — Was a larger organization behind the bombing than the four convicted terrorists? Who ordered the bombing? What was the motive for the bombing?

THE BROTHER AND THE BOYFRIEND –
THE MURDER THAT SHOULDN'T HAVE HAPPENED

It was Thursday, January 14, 1993 in Los Angeles. On this dry, sunny morning David decided to take his car, a black 1968 Chrysler, to the shop to have it tuned. It had been acting up recently and nobody in Los Angeles can be without wheels, especially as he had an audition the next day. As he stood outside the shop, a red BMW whizzed by and then backed up.

Allen, his girlfriend's brother, sat glaring at him. "Listen, kid, keep away from my sister, or I'll see to it that you never mess around with her again. And I'm not kidding — I'll put a hole in your brain."

David didn't care much for Allen. He was six foot six, darkly handsome, and had a crazy reputation. Reputedly, Allen was a computer genius, but he only worked sporadically and spent his money on fast cars and flashy, expensive clothes. The women he took out were usually one-night stands. The only woman Allen really cared for was his sister, Polly, who was something else again. She was tall, independent, and gorgeous, with long legs and long blond hair.

David couldn't believe his luck when Polly told him she would move in with him. That hadn't happened yet, partly, David suspected, because of her

David Murder Victim

Jan 31 1966   3:30 PM CST
Chicago   Illinois
41N51   87W39
Jan 31 1966   21:30:00 GMT
Tropical   Placidus   True Node

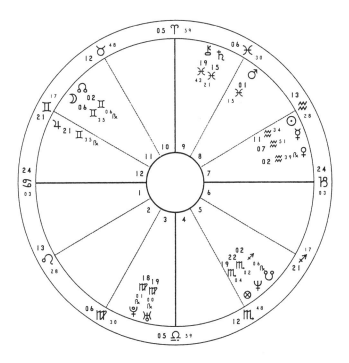

brother Allen, who had something sinister about him. But David wasn't happy with his digs, which he rented from another pair of aspiring actors. He had just one room in a rather funky townhouse in the hills, with used couches and futons on dusty floors. He hoped to get enough money to move some place more suitable for a wonderful girl like Polly, but jobs were few and far between.

Clouds had moved in by the time they had finished with his car, which cost more than he ex-

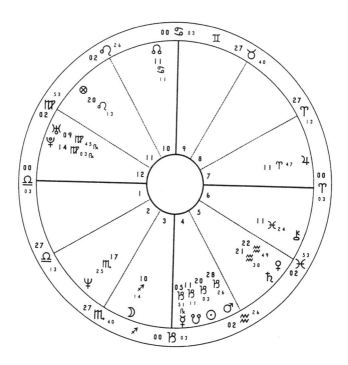

Allen

Jan 10 1964   10:34 PM PST
Los Angeles   California
34N03   118W15
Jan 11 1964   06:34:00 GMT
Tropical   Placidus   True Node

pected, so he decided to skip lunch. It also had turned chilly, like fall back east, and he needed a sweater. His landlord, Gene, with whom he had gone to school at New York University where they both studied film editing, had a job with a talent agent and had arranged the appointment.

When he got home, Sue, who lived with Gene and whom David had also known at NYU, was fixing a sandwich of left-over meatloaf. She made one for him, too. He and Sue had once had a brief relationship.

Polly
Mar 16 1966   11:23 PM PST
Los Angeles   California
34N03   118W15
Mar 17 1966   07:23:00 GMT
Tropical   Placidus   True Node

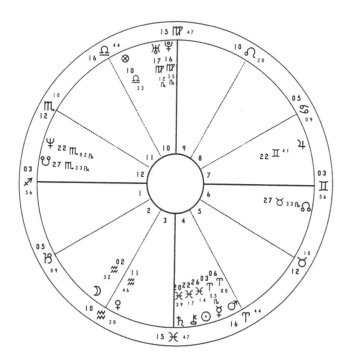

When he told her about Allen's threat, Sue made a face. She didn't care much for Polly and she thought her brother was a creep. "Stay away from them both," she told him. But David just shook his head. He couldn't stay away from Polly.

He worked on his tapes until it got dark and decided to go out for fast food. When he looked at his watch it was after ten. David's father was generous; he kept sending David his allowance "'til you get on your feet," but David was careful about spending much on himself. He saved for dates with Polly, although she made good money as a model and was generous about sharing expenses.

He grabbed his leather jacket, a Christmas present from his father, and locked it in the trunk — the jacket was new and if he went into the restaurant, he didn't want anyone to take it. Then he was about to get behind the wheel when a car turned into the driveway and he was blinded by its lights. Before he could move or duck away, a shot gun blew a hole in his chest.

His watch showed the time he died — exactly 10:14 p.m.. The sign of the zodiac rising over the horizon at that moment was changing from Virgo to Libra. And Polly's brother, Allen, who had Libra rising, raced away from the murder scene and kept driving north, away from the city. He had a head start on the police because the body wasn't discovered until the next morning.

Sue and Gene had been watching television and neither heard the shot, although later Sue told the police that she had heard a noise but thought it was a car backfiring. They finished their TV show and went to bed. David's room was dark so they figured he had gone to bed early because of his audition. They didn't discover David's body until the next morning when Gene was leaving for work. He was late — and life must go on — so he told Sue to call the police.

These young people were all in their mid-twenties. But they were young for their age, pampered by indulgent families. Sue wanted what she considered a grown-up and remembered that David had gone to Christmas dinner last year with a friend of his father's, a Mrs. Overton. She hunted frantically among David's old things and finally found an address book. A Laurel Overton was listed in Pasadena.

She called and — blessed relief — a woman answered. A cool, take charge voice it was, and Sue almost wept with relief. Laurel, whoever she was, seemed upset but she did not panic. She told Sue to stay put, she would call the police and come as fast as she could.

When Laurel Overton arrived, one young policeman was trying to keep some curious. kids away. It was starting to rain and, over the objections of the cop, she put her raincoat over David's body. Then she went inside to find Sue in hysterics. Sue blurted out the story — Allen had already threatened David for fooling around with his sister, Polly, so Allen had shot him. "I always knew Polly was bad news."

"Have you told her about David?"

"No. Why should I?"

"She might know where her brother is. Call her."

Sue came back from the telephone, "She's coming over. She doesn't know where Allen is. He didn't come home last night but that's nothing unusual."

The young cop tried to detain Polly, but he was no match for her. She stormed into the house. Both girls started screaming at each other. Laurel went outside with the cop and waited for the detectives. Two of them finally arrived. She explained to them that she was a friend of the family and had known David since he was born. They tried to talk to Sue and Polly but finally settled on what Laurel had to say — that Polly's brother had probably been the culprit and that he was missing. They managed to get Allen's address and a description of him from Polly and loaded David's body into the van.

It seemed to be routine for the police. They informed Laurel that there were lots of shootings in these hills, "Mostly crazy kids high on speed. But we'll send out a description and try to find him."

There was no gun in sight so they would impound the car as evidence. Before they left, Laurel wrote down their names, telephone numbers, and precinct numbers in her notebook. Then she went home to call David's father, Brian Kean, in Chicago. And that is how I came into it.

Brian Kean is my client. Four years ago, in the midst of getting a divorce, he had come to me for help. I had done his chart and told him everything would be resolved in less than three months, there were favorable aspects ahead for him. It happened exactly as I saw the indications, which seemed to him miraculous. Then he asked me to do the chart of his son, David, the youngest of three children. "I don't worry about the girls, ever. But David has always seemed to be floundering. He's in New York now going to NYU film school and he wants to be either a musician or an actor but I don't think he has the talent to be either. I hate to discourage him but he doesn't have his feet on the ground. "

I had studied David's chart — I never saw him, of course — and it defied interpretation because there was so little in it. Most charts "speak" to me and immediately give me the outline of a story for me to interpret, much like the outline of a playscript.

But David's chart was scattered. It showed interests, many of them, and a few talents, but nothing definite and strong. I remember feeling that his father was disappointed in what I found because it was all general and inconclusive, but I couldn't help it. I recalled that I had suggested the year 1993 would be a turning point, perhaps a "new beginning," because his progressed sixth house cusp would then join natal Mars and square the nodes of the moon at birth. Problems!

It is difficult to be sure of a death in a chart, for so often, as I've said before, the indications can mean a change in one's life, for better or worse. And I wasn't looking for trouble because at that moment his father had his fill of it.

In retrospect — we always are so wise in retrospect — if I had known that David would go to Hollywood to seek fame and fortune, I could have warned that he would be disappointed. I could even have told him he was risking his life.

We have charts of cities, mathematically calculated for the times of incorporation and/or the time of its foundation — such as a Spanish settlement, as is the case for Los Angeles. And, comparing David's chart with that of Los Angeles, there were several specific indications of trouble waiting for him. Saturn, in the Los Angeles chart, blocked the Uranian creativity in David, depressing him. The Los Angeles south node of the moon (karma) threatened David's ascendant (his life span) and the Los Angeles Pluto was in Aquarius sitting on David's Venus and sun. Emotional problems.

But I had not studied David's chart for four years. I never saw him, so I had not progressed his chart this far ahead! If I had, I could have seen that in January 1993, his progressed moon would square his natal Mars. Trouble! Death? Maybe. Could we have stopped it? Not likely. Destiny is too strong. The best we could have done would have been to warn him — and to do that would have worried him!

Laurel Overton had arranged to have David's body shipped to Chicago where Brian and his daughters planned a funeral service and burial in the family plot. He called me after the service and asked if he could come to see me and find some explanation before he went out to Los Angeles to pick up David's possessions and see the police.

I told him that if his friend Laurel could possibly

find the factors — I needed time, place, and date of birth for the girl Polly and her brother — I would compare their charts and explore the astrological aspects. But until I did that, all I could tell him was that David should never have gone to Los Angeles!

Brian said, "I tried to stop him but his friends Gene and Sue were there — and you know how kids are. Laurel has met both girls and I'm sure she'll get what you want. She used to be a reporter for the *Los Angeles Times* and knows her way around. She resigned two years ago to take care of her husband, who had cancer. Since his death, she's been freelancing."

"How did you get to know her?"

"Her mother, widowed very young, was registrar at Northwestern and was a friend of my mother's. Laurel always wanted to be a reporter — she worked as campus correspondent for the *Tribune* before she graduated and landed a job on the staff afterwards. We always kept in touch and she knew my kids when they were young. She married a man from Los Angeles and moved out there ten or eleven years ago. But we wrote and phoned, especially after David was out there."

I said I thought Laurel sounded like a woman who would produce results. Two days later, she called me on the telephone to say, "I gave Brian this information but he thought it would be better if I could talk to you directly. He doesn't say much, but he's very depressed.

"I've met Polly, the girl David was dating — Allen's sister. She's pretty far out, but I liked her. Very attractive. Blonde, almost six foot.

"But tattooed all over her body — told me she had worn her former boyfriend's name until she met David, who asked her to have it removed. She did, and now she's having the names David and Polly intertwined in red and black tattooed on her arm. She must truly have cared about him."

She continued, "Through her study of astrology, Polly had come to understand why she seemed to play the man's role more than he — even with her sun in Pisces — because she had two and one half degrees of Sagittarius on the ascendant, seeking excitement, fascinated by the unknown, but cooling when the challenge loses its excitement. David, on the other hand, had Cancer rising, making him the nourishing one of the pair. Sensitive, caring, tender. Polly told Laurel how they were trapped in an ugly situation once, in a violent fracas in a public place in San Francisco — and it was Polly who punched out the offending tough guys who started the trouble!

"So it was almost as though she played the masculine role in their relationship, and he the feminine counterpoint. It seemed natural, and she loved him for it.

"Her mother died when she was two. Her brother Allen was four and watched his mother suffer of cancer. He never got over it. When their father married again, to a woman who tried to take care of them, Polly was grateful but Allen went into rages. He was about eight years old then, a big boy who looked older. His stepmother was afraid of him. So his father sent him to military school. One night he tried to burn down the barracks.

"The father and stepmother gave up trying to discipline him and let Allen go to public high school where he did rather well. He was smart in class and became a star on the basketball team. But at UCLA he felt lost in a big pond and dropped out. Too bad, because he has writing talent. And then another tragedy, not so long ago. His father was killed. The police had surrounded the house in a raid because he was selling guns and they knew he was armed. They broke in and he was killed when a statue fell and crushed his skull.

"This was about eight or nine years ago. So you see the tragic picture here. Pretty sordid. He lost both mother and father, and Polly was all he had. To please him, when he moved into a place in the hills, she joined him. But she's a flirt and David was a nice-looking boy — so they became a couple."

"Brian said he thought they were engaged."

"No way. She offered to move in once, but she was not a girl to be tied down. And she knew how much it would hurt her brother if she moved out. David was a dreamer, poor boy. Polly doesn't want to belong to anyone, even David. She liked his sweetness and innocence — as did we all — yet she knew it would be soon over for her, and she hoped he wouldn't be too hurt. They loved playing together and made plans for the future. Yet she wondered if it would really last! After all they both had the Geminian moon which is usually a form between two!

"Who knows? Allen had sense enough to run away, and he was helped by the fact the police didn't get on the case until the next day and they don't work weekends except on big cases. If he's as smart as Polly said, they may never catch him. Besides, the police aren't breaking their necks. They don't worry much about these hill kids."

I thanked her and said I would try to find some rationale when I compared the charts. She said, "I hope so. Brian is taking it very hard. He doesn't deserve the things that have happened to him, he's too nice a guy."

I hung up, thinking that Laurel was half in love with Brian. If so, it was what he needed at this time in his life and he was due for a change.

Brian was not going to be back until the end of the month, so I kept a Sunday free and sat home with the charts. David was born January 31, 1966, at 3:30 p.m. in Chicago. He had his sun in Aquarius, Cancer rising, and moon in Gemini, explaining the attraction to Polly, who also had a Gemini moon.

Allen, her bother, was born January 10, 1964, in Los Angles. Sun in Capricorn, moon in Scorpio, and Libra rising — the same sign which was rising over the horizon on January 14 at the very moment David was shot, changing from Virgo to Libra. Libra requires balance, and Allen had Libra rising. He needed to balance the scales of his life and this is what he thought he was doing when he shot David, eliminating this conflict which bothered him. A silly thought — he was only making things worse. But he was a mixed-up young man. He had twenty-four degrees of Libra rising which is a degree of obsessive pride and jealousy.

He was in a confused and troubled state. His inability to work things out, to balance his love for his sister, and his jealousy of David, impelled him to do something to resolve his destiny, balance the scales. His overpowering emotions pointed to only one solution, get rid of David. David had a loving family of his own, a devoted father and two sisters. He didn't need Polly — but Allen did desperately.

He was unable to think or reason. He was cursed with the burden that he had carried since birth. He was born during the dark of the moon and a solar eclipse occurred four days later. His life has been a series of hurts and disappointments.

In early spring of 1966, when he was two years old, Allen's Libra ascendant squared his Mars, the planet of sex and violence, anger and resentment, jealousy. That is when his sister Polly was born, and obsessive love came into his life with its feelings of intense jealousy and desire, expressed by his eighth house cusp (karma) picking up the moon; which represents the most influential woman in a man's life. Mars brought a heavy burden into his life, under which he suffered without being able to recognize the cause.

This picture was again inflamed by something that happened in the early summer of 1968, when he was four. It was then that Allen saw his mother suffer, which left emotional scars that would never heal. The destructive planetary influence in this case was Saturn joined to Venus, where it literally squashes the loving nature of Venus and the joy it usually brings, leaving in its wake the frustration and disappointment that was to follow him through his life.

When his father remarried — the event is indicated in his chart again in the early seventies — more trauma was unleashed. His powerful moon in twenty-nine degrees of Scorpio pushed him into violence. The last answer in the world for this disturbed boy was the discipline of military school.

As a boy, Allen was already a mine field of planetary fireworks, about to shoot off wildly in any direction. When the explosion finally came in 1993, David was the victim. Polly, born March 16, 1966, at 11:23 p.m. in Los Angeles — sun in Pisces, her moon in capricious Gemini, and Sagittarius rising. Her Neptune on Allen's moon put him under her spell; she was different from ordinary girls, almost as tall as he (six feet), feminine yet independent, flirtatious yet with a deep need for freedom. She was a survivor — her chart showed her clever and resourceful. That was lucky because she would probably be tested all her life. She loved her brother but she never had needed him.

That is what was so frustrating to Allen, fascinating and confusing him. He needed her and wanted her to need him. But that wasn't in her nature. And so he brooded, as Scorpios are want to do. Secretly nursing his wounds and his desires, which were deeply hidden, the burden was intolerable. Was he sexually attracted to his sister? Probably. Her Jupiter opposes his Mars (sex) and his Mars squared her Venus. This means sensual attraction — incest which festered in him, unresolved.

And it all exploded on the night of January 14, 1993 in Los Angeles at 10:14. Yet everything could have been different. Anyone with a powerful moon in twenty-nine degrees of Scorpio could perform something outstanding if controlled directly and constructively, and dissuaded from violence. And if David hadn't stubbornly insisted on going west — bad karma — he wouldn't have stepped into Allen's line of fire. *It was a murder that shouldn't have happened.*

Brian called me after his return and asked me to dinner. I suggested that he pick me up at my place where we could talk in private first. Then I told him what I had seen in the three charts.

When we got to the restaurant he asked for a table in the back where it was quiet. After we ordered, he said, "In light of what you have told me, I think you'll be interested in what I found in Los Angeles.

"Laurel wanted me to stay with her, but I needed to face this alone. She booked me into a nice motel near her and I rented a car at the airport. I got there on Friday because I wanted to see Gene when he didn't have to work. And I drove out to his place the next day. There was a sort of village with a lot of queer old houses, most of them falling down. Gene's place was no better and no worse. But it was depressing, terribly. The kids tried their best to be nice — Gene kept repeating over and over how awful it was and how upset he and Sue were — but that didn't help me.

"They had packed his clothes in two cartons and there was a suitcase with his camera and a lot of tapes and cassettes. I said I'd take the suitcase, but couldn't someone use his clothes? Gene allowed they were probably too big for him but he had friends that might. The one thing he would like was David's black leather jacket. It wasn't in his room and if I found it, he'd appreciate that."

The waiter put food in front of us and Brian raised his wine glass to me. "I appreciate all you've done. It gives me a perspective I didn't have before."

During the rest of the dinner, he told his story. After he had left the hills, he had called Laurel and she had insisted he come to dinner, she had a fire going and she knew he needed to talk. That night — she had said she had David's car — the police had released it — and it was in her garage. She had suggested waiting until the next day to see it.

Brian had agreed. He had had all he could stand that day. But he had slept well and the next morning the sun had been shining and he had felt better. Laurel had showed him the car. He was glad he had waited because it was a bit of a shock. Before the police had impounded it, the kids had held some kind of a service in it. The dashboard and back seat had been covered with dead roses and there was a pungent sweet smell of something else — Laurel had suggested it was Petouli oil, which some of the young people seemed to like. Brian continued,"Laurel said, 'I knew this might upset you but I didn't clean it out because I wanted you to see that the three of them — including Polly — cared about David. Now I'll help you.'"

When they had finished, he had opened the trunk

and found David's leather jacket. Laurel had suggested they drop it off at Gene's house after they saw the police.

The police visit had been as futile as he had feared. Only one of the detectives on the case had been on duty and he had reported that they had issued a warrant for a felony arrest and that the FBI was interested but, so far, no leads. "These kids disappear into the woodwork."

"Allen was pretty noticeable. He was six feet six and well built," Laurel had objected. The detective had smiled. He remembered Laurel had told him she used to be on the *Times*. "Newspapers think we have eyes everywhere. We don't. I'm sorry, folks — we'll let you know if we get anything."

Brian smiled at me. "That's the whole story. It's over. I have mixed feelings about hunting Allen down like a criminal. Of course he killed David but it wasn't in cold blood, he was a troubled boy. He hated poor innocent David for stupid reasons. You told me you saw something in David's chart four years ago that told of a change, a new beginning. Poor kid, I wish it had been a happier new life for him. I hope I didn't fail him."

"You did everything you could. No parent should hang on to his or her children — they need freedom to live their own lives."

He drank coffee and looked into space. Poor man, I knew this was something he would never get over. Time, however, works wonders, softens blows. And Brian had reached a turning point in his life, the positive results of Saturn returning in the age cycle of 56 to 59. I said, "Your chart suggests that it's time to start a new pattern. Are you thinking of getting married?"

Silence. That old familiar curtain dropped again. I didn't pursue the suggestion, for I knew he wasn't ready. We left the restaurant and parted soon after.

A year passed before I saw him again. But that wasn't surprising. It was his pattern, a part of his nature. Occasionally I thought about him, knowing what he was going through. I knew he would be suffering, unable to talk about it, to share his emptiness with anyone. I knew what it was like because I had gone through it when my husband died.

Then one night, just as I was getting ready for bed, he called. Apologizing for the late hour, he said he had been with a group of friends and my name came up when astrology was mentioned. He said, "I realized I needed to see you. Is that possible?"

I gave him an appointment that very week, because I was curious. When he came in, he seemed as usual. Or did he? He looked different. Sad, yes, but different. Serious, but he had always been that. Brian is another Piscean. He was born early in March, close to noon, with Gemini rising, like his son.

When I had first seen him as a client years ago, I knew I wasn't getting through the protective screen that so many Geminis put up. In his case, I was sure he felt he had to hide his sensitive Pisces nature to avoid being hurt. In various ways, I tried to reach him, but his resistance defeated me — he was the Pisces fish who swam away to come again another day! Finally, I decided he either did not actually have the depth I thought I detected or he was never going to reveal it.

But now — now the difference was that the protective screen had dropped. He was sad, yet strangely calm, almost tranquil. Acceptance of pain had changed his mien, his aura. He started out telling me of another recent death — of his closest man-friend, not long after David's murder.

Grief had changed him, yes. And it had done something more. It had forced him to seek deeply within himself for the insecurities which had festered inside him all of his life. What is more, he wanted to talk. Then he showed me a letter David had written to him three years before, in 1991, a birthday greeting to his father — the only letter David had ever written to him. He had been pleased and touched at the time, but now, since David's death, he was able to comprehend fully what David had been trying to tell him.

Brian was a successful architect. And, as so many fathers did in the post-Depression era, he wanted his children to have everything — and that requires money. He built a house in Lake Forest — a big one — and indulged them with everything material — fancy bikes, cars, a boat. He confessed to me that even when he was earning big money, he felt inferior to his multi-millionaire neighbors. Now, as he read and re-read his son's letter, he was able to see where he had gone wrong.

He told me, "David loved me, and because he loved me, he wanted to tell me to relax and find happiness in life, instead of thinking only of how much money I could make. And he was so right. Now that he is gone, I see it so clearly."

He let me read the letter. It was a loving and enchanting letter, written in a script very like his father's. And with his father's permission, I am sharing some of it with you:

"Dear Dad,

"I will never understand why you can't see yourself as the great success story that we all see. Every person who crosses your path goes away thinking, 'What a great guy.' All my girlfriends have had (probably still do) a crush on you. Your whole life has provided humor and good times to everyone you meet. And that's what success means. To have so many people look up to you and enjoy

your company is a truly successful person. Everyone wants to have more money. But realize that money is just one element of a person's life. And besides, you've made plenty of it — enough to set the three lives of your kids on the path of good fortune. And one day, we may be shooting pool in my slick new Hollywood villa (or, more likely, the two of us shooting pool in my sister, Lisa's, rec room). So now is the time to spoil yourself; with all your new toys, your quick wit and freedom, you can have all the top-shelf women of Chi-town at your feet. The world is your oyster, so swallow it."

When I looked up from the letter, there were tears in my eyes. "A voice from the grave," he said.

I nodded. "What I see is that your son David is actually taking over your life as a guide, a father figure. This was true in his life on earth, although you were not as deeply receptive as you are now. David's Jupiter on your ascendant is significant. David, young as he was, with his sun in Aquarius, was a born teacher. Jupiter is a gift — a gift of the spirit! He is with you now, helping you realize that material views should not be first, as they used to be. You never were selfish, you did it to provide for your family."

He said, slowly, "I know now that I had to suffer deeply — both from David's death and that of my friend's, before I came really alive, aware of what I can give, but not in material terms. My talents as a builder can be used to benefit others. For the first time in my life, I feel really alive."

What he has experienced is the beauty that can be gleaned from tragedy. Grief is a learning process and suffering opens our eyes to the real values.

Meanwhile, Brian tells me David's friends are changing — giving up bad habits, going off drugs and alcohol as a tribute to his memory. And once in a while, when I think of David, it seems as though the fragrance of dead roses permeates the room!

Update at press time: Would the police ever find Allen? Everyone wanted to know, and when Brian asked what showed in the chart, I had to tell him I couldn't find anything to indicate he would be caught — certainly not soon. However, in a year and a half he might receive some news about the case.

And that is just what happened. Caught? Yes, if you want to call it that. There was a solar eclipse at almost twenty degrees of Taurus in the eighth house of Allen's chart on May 10, 1994 (often called the "house of death") exactly squaring his progressed sun which was right on his natal Saturn, suggesting death! At the same time, in June-July '94, his progressed moon joined the natal sun — a progressed new moon, which means a new beginning!

The police found his old demolished pick-up truck down the side of a steep hill — a skeleton with skull was inside. It had been there a long time and investigation proved it to be Allen's. Allen had told his sister that he would shoot David and kill himself. Apparently he kept his word.

THE CHINESE PUZZLE

One of my favorite clients is Gordon Sinclair who conceived one of Chicago's most glamorous gourmet restaurants, Gordon. He will not hire a chef, a manager, nor consider a business move without consulting me, and having me check the charts of those involved compared with his. That has worked so well that recently he called to tell me that he was considering choosing a doctor and would I do his chart?

I said, concerned, for Gordon is always on the go, "Are you ill?"

"No, but I want someone to take care of me tenderly in my old age."

I did a horoscope for the doctor, who was in his late thirties, and reported to Gordon that they were a good pair. Then I couldn't help asking, "Did he have you consult me?"

Gordon is on the cusp between Gemini and Cancer. The people born on that particular cusp are often difficult to understand because they can be changeable emotionally, even occasionally moody. But they are so bright — Mercury, the mind, is the guiding planet of Gemini and the fast-moving moon rules Cancer. They are so quick to grasp every situation. I could see his mind racing to answer before I even broached the question. "Of course not. I told him

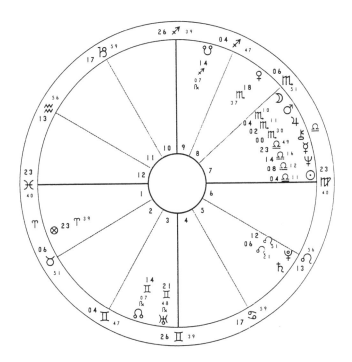

Helena Martin

Sep 27 1946	6:17 PM EDT
Manhattan	New York
40N46	73W59
Sep 27 1946	22:17:00 GMT
Tropical	Placidus True Node

that if you don't have an astrological chart, you are going through life without a compass. He was so impressed he wants to come and see you and have you do his horoscope."

I was not surprised because Gordon is habitually sending me clients he thinks need my help. A number of years ago, when I still had my studio in a high-rise on the Chicago river, he sent me a beautiful young woman who was part Chinese and part American. It was the middle of a bad, stormy day, but she was so elegant in her appearance she could have stepped off a fashion runway. She casually draped her sable coat, which must have cost many thousands of dollars, on a chair and sat down opposite me.

"My name is Helena Martin, but please call me Helena. I was at Gordon's one night with my fiancé, Ted Kiam, and I told Mr. Sinclair we were trying to pick a date for Ted to take me to Hong Kong and introduce me to his mother. Mr. Sinclair said he knew the perfect person to help me, so here I am."

"It sounds like a great adventure."

"Yes." She seemed hesitant. "But she is a very formidable lady and he is her elder son. She wants him to marry well and I am only part Chinese."

Two things occurred to me as she spoke. She was obviously not as materialistic as the clothes indicated. The second was that one evening when I was dining at Gordon there was a large table of people headed by a meticulously groomed Chinese man who was obviously entertaining in lavish style. I didn't remember Helena — all the women were beautifully dressed — but I did remember the arrogant manner he had with the waiters. "I shall need to know your place and date of birth and the exact time, if possible. I'd also like to compare it with the birth chart of your fiancé. Do you know when he was born?"

"I know the day and month, but not the year. Ted is — well, a little older than I am and he is shy about telling me his age."

"Do you happen to have a snapshot of him?"

She opened an elegant alligator bag and gave me a conspiratorial smile, "I do, but he doesn't know I took it. He is shy about having his picture taken because he has what he calls his 'corporation' — a little bit of a paunch. But it's the only one I have of him. I carry it in my bag the way other people carry snapshots of their children."

I was touched. She was obviously in love. I asked her then about her birth date. She was born September 27, 1946, in New York City, late afternoon — "in time for dinner." Her mother, an actress, had just walked out of a matinee when labor pains began. So Helena had her sun in charming Libra — I recognized the wonderful Libra smile — with Pisces rising to make her very sensitive. Her moon and Venus in Scorpio had given her a sensuous beauty and her deep brown eyes, flecked with green, those so-called "bedroom eyes" for which Scorpios are known. Helena was no clothes horse, although she wore clothes well. She was a beautiful human being, inside and out.

Her fiancé had been born in Peking, now Beijing, on November 10, but she had no idea of the year. So all I had to go on was that he had his natal sun in Scorpio. His Chinese name was Kiam Tiem-no, but he had anglicized it to Ted Kiam. Helena's father had done the same, changing her Hui-lanto to the Caucasian Helena. As it would be impossible for me to do his chart, all I had to go on was his Scorpio sun.

A man with his sun in Scorpio can create a very strong bond with a woman whose moon is in Scorpio. There's no question about it, he was the dominating force in their relationship. But what really worried me was that she had a malefic aspect to her Scorpio moon. It was joined to Venus, with Mars joined to Jupiter, all squared by a ninety-degree aspect to Pluto and Saturn in Leo. Menacing — a tricky and violent threat to her life. She would need some very strong and protective planetary influences to overcome the negative aspects which were so powerful. I was concerned. *Very!* This was something that had to be dealt with carefully.

I studied the snapshot she had given me. He was dressed in resplendent white, standing on a carefully curry-combed beach. His jacket was cleverly tailored to conceal his "corporation." He looked in robust health but I judged him to be closer to sixty than fifty — no wonder he didn't want Helena to know his real age. A good-looking man, yes. But I didn't like the look of craftiness in his deep-set eyes. They were not open to whomever he was looking at. And he was not looking out, to be friendly. He was inside himself, analyzing and conniving.

I didn't like this man, anymore than I had liked what I saw of him at the restaurant. But I couldn't tell her that. I only wondered if she had come to me to find out something more important than the date for meeting her future mother-in-law.

Most clients know that whatever I tell them is entirely private, that I would never reveal any detail of a client relationship to anyone without his or her permission. I decided to let her relax and tell me a little more about herself. She seemed delighted that I was interested.

"My mother was a popular actress in Hong Kong, very very beautiful and talented, my father said. They met when he was on an architectural assignment in Hong Kong and fell passionately in love. He could not marry her — he had a wife and a mentally retarded daughter at home — but she wanted his child, me. When I was three years old, she was killed in a train crash with many other victims. My father went to Hong Kong, adopted me, and took me back to New York City with him.

My stepmother was a very unhappy woman, with an eighteen-year old daughter who was mentally about six. It was an awkward situation, she resented me and my father's obvious delight in me. She thought he was neglecting her daughter. Finally my father had to move out and take me with him.

"I was about ten then, and he placed me in various boarding schools until I was ready for college. But we were together on holidays and vacations. I never made close friends in school but the relationship between us was wonderful. He told me about my mother and how I was his real child. And when I got out of Vassar, he bought an apartment on the river and we lived together, very happily, until he developed pancreatic cancer — inoperable. It was all over in a few months."

There were tears in her dark eyes though she still gave me that wonderful smile.

I had to ask, "How long ago did he die?"

"It will be five years next June, just before Father's Day. I was shattered. He had done the right thing — divided his estate in three parts, one to his wife, one to each of his daughters. The lawyer suggested I put the money he had left me — it was quite a substantial sum — into an annuity. But I couldn't bring myself to do it, sensible as it might be. I didn't want to set something aside for my old age. I wanted to live now. Do you understand?"

I did, indeed. Her Scorpio planets made her unafraid, ready for adventure and challenge. I wondered if her progressed ascendant had lead her into a relationship with Ted Kiam. So I asked her how she met him. And I got a happy smile in return.

"A friend who had known my father a long time, a Mrs. Malcolm, came to the service and was very nice to me — I think she had kind of a crush on my father. Anyway, she quite agreed with me that instead of buying an annuity, I should have some adventure in my life. She knew a wonderful Chinese investment counselor who handled her finances and she was sure he would do well by me."

Adventure, I thought, the unafraid Scorpio moon

which walks into the lion's den without flinching.

"And you liked him?"

"He was unlike anyone I had ever seen. He was so immensely wealthy and yet — so much fun. He told me any fool could make money, what he wanted was to use it to do things and go places, have a wonderful life.

"He was in New York on business, although his home base is Chicago. He was staying at the Waldorf Towers, where all the heads of state go. I was still in mourning — I must have looked pretty drab — because after we talked about investments and he assured me that he would make sure I would never have to worry about money, he said, 'I want to take you out to dinner tonight, someplace where we can dance. But first I want you to do me a favor. Come to Bergdorf's with me. Some men send their dates flowers. I am going to buy you the most beautiful dress in New York'.

"I protested that I was in mourning. But he took me by the hand, like a little girl. We got in a cab and he took me up to Bergdorf's where he had all the models parading in front of us. Suddenly, he stopped one, saying, 'That's for you.' And I went and tried it on. It was like the prince discovering Cinderella. That's the kind of magic he brought into my life." She hesitated, then corrected herself, "brings into my life.

"He had to go back to Chicago but he called me every morning and night. He said that I was too far away, he wanted me where he could see me everyday. He found me a beautiful apartment here and arranged to sell the one my father had bought at a very good price. Then he arranged charge accounts for me in all the best stores here and told me to buy anything I wanted, he would see that there was plenty of money to pay for everything, and he wanted me to look as beautiful and well-groomed as the wives of his business associates whom I was going to meet. And he always introduced me as his fiancée but said that he could not marry me until I went with him to Hong Kong to meet his mother and get her approval.

"I've been raised as an American, and to me the idea that a grown-up man would have to ask his mother for permission to marry was pretty silly. But then he scolded me, told me I had been seduced away from my Chinese heritage.

"That was as near an argument as we had ever had. I went home hurt, and the next morning he didn't give me what he called his usual wake-up call. I spent a bad day, remembering how good he was to me, how generous, how he had given me the kind of life most women only dream about, giving me everything I wanted. It wasn't so much the money — it was the thought, the generosity. He is that way with everybody, all the girls in his office. He is always giving them presents, entertaining them. I called him and apologized. And then it was much as usual.

"Only he kept saying he couldn't marry me until his mother approved, it was necessary. Even men of middle age always kow-towed to their mothers. Then we began talking about when we would go to Hong Kong, when it would be convenient for his business. And it was all such a muddle I broke down and confessed to Mr. Sinclair one night. Do you understand why I want you to pick a good time?"

"Was this your fiancé's idea?"

"No, not exactly. One night at the restaurant, I was early and Mr. Sinclair took me to a table and sat down with me. To make conversation, I told him the difficulty about finding a good date. When Ted arrived, he nodded and said seeing you would be a good idea."

"Why are you so afraid about meeting his mother?"

"I am not a full Chinese. He says these days that is not as important as love. But I'm not so sure."

"Have you considered what you might do if his mother forbids the marriage?"

"I've thought about it, yes. I guess I would go back to New York. One of the nice girls in Ted's office is leaving and he gave a party for her. She is going to New York to work in a modeling office. She told me that I would make a good model because I have the bones for it. I just don't know."

For once, there was no smile. Whether she knew it or not — I suspected she did — there was something very wrong in her relationship with this man. And one thing I was certain of — the astrological picture was bad. She had the progressed moon joining the progressed Mars in the eighth house. Every astrologer recognizes the significance of this moon position — it means the end of an old situation, or the beginning of a new one. And it meant trouble — *real trouble!*

That is what is always certain. Sometimes it means a dramatic shift in one's career. Sometimes it means an accident, break in health. Or in personal life, or divorce. Sometimes it is a combination of things in the course of transition — a divorce, a new life in another city or country. In her case, I needed to find out — does it mean the end of life? The beginning of a new one? There was also a threatening aspect from Pluto, the sometimes planet of death.

The answer depends upon many other factors in the chart. And everything I saw in hers looked ominous. I was trying not to sound grim. I gave her several dates which looked dangerous for which I wanted her to avoid any precipitous action. Then I had to warn her that there were disturbing elements around her, that someone was unfriendly, trying to trip her. But I did promise her that her chart showed she would be starting a new life — which I privately hoped would not be one in another world.

I saw a similar aspect in Diana Barrymore's chart some years before. The transition in her case meant that she could stop drinking and build herself a new career — or her death. In Barrymore's case, the transition was death.

It is not as easy to be sure of the time of death in a horoscope as some people not deep into astrology might think. Each case is different, since death has a different significance in every life. Sometimes it is a release. Sometimes it means a happy reunion with a loved one, sometimes it marks the end of a career in this life. There are many different planetary aspects which can mean transition but not necessarily death.

All I could tell her was that in a few weeks she would be in danger when an eclipse would hit her progressed moon-Mars in the eighth house. I was going to California for two weeks to visit friends and clients and I asked her to call and come to see me when I returned — so that she'd come in before the turning point would be imminent.

That was all I could do. I hoped the transition would not be what I feared. And I suggested that she make no more plans to visit Kiam's mother in Hong Kong until she saw me again.

She either did not grasp the implications of what I had said — for which I was thankful, for her peace of mind — or she already had distrust and suspicion in her heart so that what I said only confirmed what she had feared. I didn't know the answer but I worried about her while I was away. And when I returned and found she had not called for an appointment, I became concerned.

My deepest hope had been that somehow the worst could be avoided. I had no address for her and, when I called Gordon, he reported that he hadn't seen either her or Kiam for some time and had assumed they had gone to Hong Kong.

I got out her chart and studied it. There was the new moon coming up, triggering a solar eclipse opposite her progressed Mars in Scorpio on the eighth house cusp: Accident? Death? I went to bed that night, trying to figure out how I could reach her.

It was too late. The next day, there was a small story buried on one of the inside pages of the *Chicago Tribune* about an accident in one of the parking garages I had always hated because I thought it was dangerous. A woman driving a Mercedes had plunged from the fifth floor to the street. The woman had been killed instantly and she was identified by her driver's license as Helena Martin of New York City.

I was sick at heart. I could not reach Gordon — he had flown to San Francisco on business. I could only guess what could have happened. This kind of spiral parking lot always had bothered me — cars come so swiftly up the ramp and then swing into position facing outward overlooking the street five floors below with just one horizontal guard rail. (This garage has since been replaced.) Was it possible that she had stepped on the accelerator instead of the brake? Or, could someone have tampered with the car so that it looked like an accident?

I had no way of knowing. Or finding out. And, since she was dead, there was no use in thinking about it. But, knowing how alone she had been, I was determined to go to her service, to find my own way of saying goodbye to her in her different world.

Ted Kiam was not listed in the telephone book but there was a listing for Kiam International and

I called that number. A female voice answered my call. I didn't identify myself, I just asked where the Martin services would be held, and when. I was told they were to be in a mortuary a few blocks from my office. So I hung up — still unidentified — and went on the specified afternoon.

I don't know what I had expected — in view of the way he operated I thought perhaps it would be very lavish, kind of a gangster-type of funeral. It wasn't — a relief — but the flowers were so stiff and spare. I was sorry I hadn't brought something that would have suited her, like a bunch of violets or rosebuds. The attendance was also sparse. Mr. Kiam was the only Chinese man — the Caucasian-types in dark suits were employees of the mortuary, I presumed. And there were only two Caucasian women. One was a pretty blonde who signed the register before me — she seemed to know who I was as she gave me a brief smile and told me her name was Marcia. The other Caucasian woman was older and was standing by Mr. Kiam. She said something to him and he came over to me.

I introduced myself and he studied me intently. He probably recognized that I was Helena's astrologer and he took me over to the middle-aged woman and said, "This is Mrs. Malcolm, a dear friend of Helena's."

I didn't think Helena had regarded Mrs. Malcolm as a dear friend and I had the feeling she was what some people would call "pushy." She took my arm to steer me toward a seat, but I escaped and took one next to Marcia.

The service was blessedly brief. There was no coffin — Marcia whispered she was being cremated — and the young minister, who read a few ritual passages from his Bible, obviously had no idea who Helena was.

When it was over, Marcia touched my hand and told me she had to run, she had a plane to catch, but to keep away from the Malcolm woman — she was poison. "I knew her from my health club — she used to come with an old man. She was snoopy. She found out I was a bookkeeper and my old firm had just gone into bankruptcy. She told me she knew a wonderful Chinese man who was looking for a bookkeeper who would pay my way to Chicago and offer me good money. That part was true — but he was a thief. I think she got Helena into his clutches, too. So watch out. I'll keep in touch."

I tried to escape with her, but Mr. Kiam stopped me. "Julia" — that was obviously Mrs. Malcolm — "is taking Helena's ashes back to New York to be buried beside her father. I am too desolate to accompany her. But would you have a bite to eat with us? I could do with a drink, too — a goodbye toast to Helena."

The very idea sickened me. I said I had appointments, that I had to get back. But he put his hand firmly on my wrist. "I would like to talk to you. Could I call you for an appointment?"

What choice had I? I told him I was listed in the directory. And a few days later he did indeed call to make an appointment. I didn't want to see him — I disliked the man intensely and even suspected he was dangerous — but I was curious enough to play along with him.

It wasn't as bad as I had feared. He had a teen-aged boy with him, his son by a previous marriage. Ostensibly, it was the boy he wanted me to advise about his talents, his future career, and choice of schools. It is what I do often with young people and that was simple enough. But Kiam did not leave us alone — most parents do and I prefer it — but instead sat on the chair beside the boy.

It was all very correct, the father treated me like an important, authoritative figure and the boy was equally courteous. Yet I had the feeling Kiam was furtively observing me, storing every detail in his mind, watching me like a cat for any indication that I suspected him, or knew more than I should.

I kept my English poker face and concealed whatever nervousness I couldn't help feeling. I guessed that he was worried whether Helena had told me more about him than she had. I was innocent, there was nothing to hide. I knew nothing about his financial dealings and didn't want to. I did suspect him of killing Helena — or driving her to kill herself — but I had no proof.

When I finished the boy's chart, he thanked me effusively and assured me that some day he would like me to do his horoscope. I knew it was a gesture, that he was annoyed because the visit had been fruitless. But he offered me his hand when they left and I took it, reluctantly. His hand was not clammy or moist, as I had thought it might be, but cold and guarded. That scared me more than anything — I was glad when the door closed on them.

Afterward, I said to Gordon, "I didn't have any chart to guide me, only the few facts which Helena had told me — and there was nothing incriminating in them, only in her chart. Yet I know that man, I know him for what he is, a murderer — vicious and cruel — capable of killing the girl who loved him. I saw it all in her chart, this evil man who destroyed her. He might hide from the law, he might feel safe because he had killed the woman who could have exposed him. I have planetary evidence that the man is dangerous, but what can I do? I couldn't even save Helena."

"Perhaps she is better off being rid of him," Gordon said. "Just remember — we both tried to help."

Not long afterwards, he reported that Kiam had fled to Hong Kong, just ahead of the law. That was that, I thought. Then about six months later, I had a letter enclosing a clipping from the *Wall Street Journal*. Kiam Tiem-no had been arrested and was in Federal prison serving time for a wide variety of investment fraud, embezzlement of client's funds, and tax evasion. Marcia had written a brief note saying, "He never let me see cancelled checks. He'd tell me to write out something for the rent, or a client, and I would never see it again. I thought at first he was disorganized but he even had the bank in his pocket. I just couldn't work like that — then when I told him I was going back to New York, he gave me a big farewell party. Helena was the only woman there who spoke English so I talked to her. I think she was very troubled about Kiam — I tried to get her to come to New York and try modeling. So I get an "A" for effort, but it didn't save her."

I thought that was the last of Ted Kiam in my life and I was thankful. But two seven-year Saturn cycles later, I had reason to think of him again.

I knew I was taking a chance, flying to Rome in May. There was an imminent crisis in my chart, something I had been aware of for several years, to do with my health — Uranus — probably an accident! But I love Italy and an old friend who was with the United Nations had written saying he had rented a huge flat for the month of May and was rattling around in it. "Come and share it with me. You'll have your own room and bath, your own privacy, and I can act as your chauffeur."

It was an irresistible offer. Although — sadly — I do not speak a word of the beautiful Italian language, I knew Sam would act as my interpreter. He was multi-lingual, a talented footloose character who wandered all over the world in his job and had a girl in every port. My husband had known him when he was a cub reporter in Chicago, found him amusing, and Sam had attached himself to us. Even after my husband died, I still heard from itchy-footed Sam who was always on the move, something that he loved about the job.

And when I thought about it, I decided that there was no way I could avoid this crisis and if I was in a different latitude and longitude it might be less severe. Sam was a thoughtful host — he was there when I needed him and stayed out of my way when I didn't. We shared expenses, for which I knew he was grateful because he was always broke.

On the morning of May 14, I was to have an audience with the Pope that a Catholic client had arranged. The largest astrological library in the world is in the Vatican — although it is closed to the public. It was at noon and Sam had offered to drive me there in his Fiat. I was dressed in proper black and was hurrying because I didn't want to be late. I went ahead of Sam as he locked the door.

And then it happened — the accident that was in my chart. Sam's flat was on the top, the fifth floor of the old building. There were two high-ceilinged flats on each floor and a long marble staircase from one floor to another.

I hadn't gone more than two or three steps when I slipped and my feet went out from under me. Oddly enough, I didn't panic. Born and reared in Chicago, I had slipped many times during icy winter storms and I had learned one thing while I was still a child — "keep your head up or you'll get a concussion" — I can still hear my father's warning. So I kept my head up. It was the strangest feeling, I would fall down a couple of steps, pause an instant and then slide on. It all happened quickly, but my impression was of slow motion. I had to let my left side take the brunt of the fall. Sam had hurried down the steps after me, but only caught up with me at the bottom.

"I'm lucky," I told him, who seemed more shaken than I. "Just a minute and I'll get up."

My glasses had jumped off my nose but were lying a few feet away, unbroken. That was a big plus, because I can't see very well without them. But when I tried to get up, my left leg was crushed under me.

Sam immediately took charge. He told me to stay where I was while he called an ambulance. Sam is good about knowing where and how to get help, something he learned in his old police reporter days. In unbelievably short time, I was moved onto a stretcher and in an ambulance which went screaming through the streets. I seemed to be very high up and Sam was down below.

The nearest hospital was one run by the government. It was poor, overcrowded, and noisy. Sam saw me through the preliminaries and I was shifted onto a gurney, an uncomfortable narrow steel table on wheels. Then Sam was told to go away, the doctors and nurses would take care of me and he could come back later. "There's nothing you can do," I told him. "There is no sense in both of us waiting around. And when you come, bring me something to wear besides this hot, long-sleeved dress."

Eventually a young doctor wheeled me into a dark space at the end of the corridor. My head was beginning to ache and I felt a huge lump forming on my forehead. The long day went on. No one around me spoke English. Patients streamed in, some in horrible shape, blood pouring from their wounds onto the floor. People were milling through it even as orderlies tried to mop up. My eyes felt parched and I had a horrible thirst. I tried to tell a nurse I wanted a drink but she didn't understand my dry croak. I was nearly frantic when a young Italian girl, obviously a visitor, saw my hand out, and I remembered enough Latin to whisper, "Aqua."

She brought me cup after cup of wonderfully cold water and we talked a little, with her practicing her English. Then she had to go and I was alone again. I wondered where Sam was; I felt hot and smelly, and repulsive. I tried to figure out why I had fallen. I hadn't been wearing heels. I had bought a pair of sensible low-heeled black pumps for traveling. I tried to concentrate on my chart. As the moon progressed to five degrees of Gemini, where it formed a helpful aspect, a man in a messy green gown came for me. He wheeled me through endless corridors, a bumpy ride, and into a huge elevator filled with nurses and doctors chattering in Italian. I hoped I would end up in a doctor's office, but that was not to be.

I was wheeled into a room of six women where there was what seemed to me a ferocious babble. They sounded angry and once I thought I heard the word "American." I knew I was being discussed. While the nurse undressed me and put me in a hospital robe, I felt resentment if not anger. Finally, she brought me a pill, which I swallowed not knowing what it was and not caring. Finally things quieted down and I slept. It must have been a sleeping pill and a powerful one for I wakened groggy and miserable. No nurse came to wash me. Finally, an attendant appeared and I was lifted on to another gurney and wheeled through endless bumpy corridors to surgery.

My leg wasn't broken, I gathered, but there was something wrong with my shoulder. I was bound up like a mummy while the smiling surgeon kept applauding me as though I had done something very clever. And I guess I had — the accident I had seen in my chart had not been as serious as it might have been.

By that time, the moon was in a good position in my chart and I felt more cheerful. But suddenly I realized I was ravenously hungry. I hadn't had any food since breakfast the day before. I made eating motions to the woman in the next bed but she kept shaking her head. Finally, food appeared, such as it was — a huge caldron of what looked like dirty dishwater with strings of spaghetti in it. This apparently was breakfast and lunch, so I ate it. At least it was wet and hot.

The day dragged on. The other women chattered or slept. I was wondering what had happened to Sam. It was mid-afternoon when he appeared, accompanied by our dear friend, the lovely Francesca. He had called the hospital regularly and the switchboard insisted I had been released. He knew that was impossible, so pulling his weight as a United Nations employee, he had finally reached the director of the hospital who found out where I was. I was so glad to see them, I hardly heard his complaints.

They were loaded down with gorgeous baskets of food, her wonderful homemade pasta, all sorts of fruit and fresh breads. I ate until I couldn't touch another bite. They managed to get a nurse who found the clothes I'd been wearing and Francesca took them home to be cleaned and promised to bring me something more suitable to wear home. By the time they were ready to leave, many visitors had arrived for the other women.

I leaned back and dozed, the first natural sleep since my accident. When I wakened, the other visitors had gone and it was getting dark. I smiled at the woman opposite me, a frail little person who had a trapeze over her bed. To my surprise, she smiled back. That was my first realization that these women were not alien monsters, they were people in trouble like myself .

That night I was again drugged into sleep, but morning was not so bad, as I had my beautiful bread and fruit for breakfast. I noticed the woman in the next bed watching me. She was a stocky woman with a profile like Mussolini. I tentatively offered her some grapes. She shook her head but took a small tin from the drawer of her bed table and offered a candy. I didn't want it, but I wasn't going to reject a gesture of friendship. I sucked and tried to say graciously "thank you" in Italian. I don't know what came out, but it provoked confusion.

That made her laugh. And suddenly, the whole atmosphere in the room changed. We all began to communicate in sign language and began laughing at each other. I finally began to realize that they hadn't been unfriendly that first night — just excited and curious about the new patient who seemed to be an American.

Bit by bit, using guesswork, I learned a bit about my companions — when they were born, what their problems were. Ms. "Mussolini" had broken ribs and a collapsed lung, which sounded terribly painful. The sweet little soul opposite me had a broken hip and feared she would never walk again. I suddenly felt empathy for her plight, so much worse than mine.

I have never thought of myself as a snob. But that night I realized part of my foolish resentment of these women had been that they weren't like me — they were foreigners! They didn't communicate with me — while all the time, they wanted to, to let me know they were sorry I was in pain.

That night, I had one of the sweetest experiences of my life. They had given me the strong sleeping pill, as usual, but I guess it didn't mask the pain and I was moaning in my sleep. I woke up to find Ms. "Mussolini", broken ribs, punctured lung, and all, leaning over me and whispering in my ear, "I love you." It was one of the sweetest utterances I had ever heard because it came from a woman who had just learned the words in English, so she could say them to me. I cried, not out of pain, but happiness, and kissed her.

The next day was Friday, the 17th, and the moon was joining Venus to bring me love and happiness. By using sign language, I found out that Ms. "Mussolini" was born on July 17 and the little woman with the broken hip was born the next day, July 18. I felt that we had known each other for years, and maybe we had, in a previous life. Ms. "Mussolini" had her sun on my Mercury in Cancer. Mercury is the messenger of the gods, representing the mind and communication. It governs the nervous system, and when it is harmoniously affected by another — in this case, warmed by her sun — it is obviously healing to both individuals. My client and dear friend for more than twenty-five years, comedienne Phyllis Diller, and another good friend, astrologer Michel Pazden, also were born July 17.

I had, literally, fallen into this situation by karma. These women and I had been brought together by fate to learn through a traumatic experience. It was the point in our lives when we each were in need of the electro-magnetic messages sent out by the other. We spoke the same language of love and friendship — we didn't need words. Although our lives and experiences were totally different, we were joined on the spiritual level.

I was scheduled to leave the hospital on Saturday. I was well enough to be carried up the five flights to Sam's apartment — the hairline fracture of my shoulder would take much longer to heal. The strange thing was, I didn't want to leave. When the time came, I scratched my name and address on a piece of paper and gave it to Ms. "Mussolini" and she wrote down her name and address and that of the woman with the broken hip. Some day we will see each other again. At least, I will send each of them a copy of this book. I will do it under a lovely aspect of Mercury — on a Wednesday, when we met — for Wednesday is Mercury's day, and my birth day.

I had lots of time to think after I was back at Sam's flat. He and Francesca — bless her — supplied me with food and reading material, but I had time to think. Two things troubled me. When Sam and Francesca took my clothes from the hospital, they saw what at first they thought were blood stains on them. But on second examination, it turned out not to be blood, but some kind of oily tomato sauce, thick as paint. When Sam had come home from taking me to the hospital he had examined the steps where I had fallen and there was no sign of blood or anything else. Someone had obviously wiped the steps clean.

I understood now why I had felt smelly and repulsive in the hospital — it was that awful tomato gook on my dress and shoes. And the fact that there was no remnant of it left when Sam came home showed that it had been put there to cause trouble.

Sam agreed with me but thought that it had been meant for him. "I have some lousy neighbors downstairs, Mafia or something weird. I think they want to get rid of me. Last week, a crazy woman, an American, rang my bell saying she was staying downstairs but it was terribly crowded and could I rent her a room? I said no, of course, then added I was expecting a guest. She seemed not to understand, said she wanted to see the room and tried to push past me. I wanted none of that — I simply took her by the hand and pushed her out and shut the door behind her. I'd forgotten about it until I saw that tomato sauce. It was meant for me."

I somehow didn't think so. "Have you any idea what the woman's name was?

"I don't think so — wait, it was Louise or Julia — something. I thought at the time it was such a pretty name for an old buzzard."

"Was it Julia Malcolm?"

Sam shrugged. "Anyway, after Francesca and I found the gook, I went downstairs and knocked on the door until a funny looking little guy, Italian, answered. I told him some female, some American female from his apartment had been harassing me. He said no woman there, never had been there, and I was crazy. So much for detective Sam."

"I think it was Julia Malcolm. She was associated with a Chinese man who was a crook and maybe Mafia. He was in federal prison the last I heard. But I've always been a bit afraid of him because I suspected he killed a client of mine, his mistress. He thought she had told me more than she had about his dealings."

"But how could they have found you here?"

"When I'm gone, I leave the telephone number of wherever I'm going to be with the answering service. It wouldn't take much ingenuity to find me. And although years have passed since that Chinese man and I have crossed paths, I've always felt that he would like to hurt me, if he could."

"And you think he sent this Julia creature to find you?"

"Maybe. She did a lot of deals for him and could still be working for him whether he's in jail or hiding out somewhere in China. He's a Scorpio. Scorpios never forget — they are the detectives of the zodiac."

Sam said, "If you say so."

I don't know. I never will, I guess. But at least I came out of it with a wonderful experience in the hospital. I was meant to learn from the accident and I did. Although the planet Uranus caused the trauma, it also brought me exciting new friends. Some day I'll go back and see them again.

IT HAD TO BE YOU! LOVE AND SEX
IN A CHANGING WORLD

"Love and marriage, love and marriage — go
together like a horse and carriage".
words and music by Sammy Cahn
and James Van Heusen

So went a popular song in the 1950s. But that no longer holds true. We are in an age of turmoil and a period of upheaval. The age of Aquarius — celebrated in a musical a couple of decades ago — is really *just* upon us. And Pluto (the catalyst) is in Scorpio (the sign of sex) which means that all the old ideas of sex, love, and especially marriage have changed.

The family, as a loving group interacting with each other, is fading and divorces are routine. It is affecting every one of us, in one way or another — particularly in the emotions!

As an astrologer, I see evidence of this constantly. Not a day passes without at least one client who is at the crossroads in his/her love life, marriage and/or partnership. There has been much talk and little understanding about the Aquarian Age. It is still a couple of hundred years away. Before it takes over, we are in a pattern of transition — sudden, unexpected, upsetting reversals. There is growing alienation among people and increasing self-focus.

Women no longer will put up with sexual harassment in the workplace. They want an equal voice in marriage, and to share responsibility. Many keep their maiden names or use a last name like Smith-Jones, combining both last names. And in some cases, marriage is not even discussed when couples decide to live together. If they want children, they may marry, or maybe not. And no longer does an unmarried woman feel any stigma if she has a child without a husband.

Never before have so many women attained high office. Although salaries still tend to lag behind those of men, this is in the process of changing. The word POWER has become almost a cliché in the vocabulary of the newly assertive woman. She wants self-fulfillment. She is tired of living in a man-made world, rejected by men-only clubs and occupations. Women head governments, attain high office (there are two women on the supreme court) and a woman jockey recently won the Kentucky Derby.

In the Age of Aquarius, love will relinquish the intensity of intimate companionship. It will be impersonal, less individual, more general — the love of humanity. And as this change approaches, we have confusion. And that is what I see in my clients — men and women.

Let me tell you about two clients, women who seem to have similar problems. One is Christine who is in her early thirties, a successful fundraiser, active in politics and women's causes. For five years, she has been living with Jason, a researcher who has his own business. She is a double Gemini with Leo rising. He is a mathematical genius, is deeply interested in music and knowledgeable about it. They have an inventive sex life and both love to dance. But the seven-year crisis in love and partnership is fast approaching. Chris has decided they should get married because she wants a child.

Jason, long divorced, with two children he seldom sees because they are in Italy with their mother, is reluctant. He is fond of Christine, deeply fond, but he backs away from commitment. Wary, he doesn't even want to discuss it. He has a Gemini moon reflecting her sun. Although they are so different in temperament — he enjoys figures and she is action-oriented — they get along, until the subject of marriage comes up. He not only runs away from it, he also runs away from her.

Recently, he fled to Albuquerque where he wrote her, "Chris, I want my independence. I have to find myself. I just can't go on with this relationship." Chris came to me close to tears. "We fit so well. My friends like him. He is talented and with my help he could be more successful. We could have such a good life. But he's stubborn — should I tell him to get lost?"

I almost said, "You already have," because I remembered a lively holiday party given by a mutual friend when they were also invited. Jason was giving a rather mathematical analysis of a music festival they had attended in Massachusetts. Chris heard him and immediately leaned over to give her version of the event. Her description was much more vivid and amusing than his. She wound up to a hilarious finish. But Jason didn't laugh and neither did I.

Afterward, my hostess told me privately, "Those two will never make it. She's a remarkable girl and an asset to any party but he's afraid of her. Why can't she realize that?" When I tried to explain to Chris that without realizing it, she comes on too strong for Jason, her reply was, "But that's the way I am. I can't change my spots."

And that is exactly why, a few months later, they broke up by mutual consent. For Chris can't change her spots and Jason feels threatened. Chris either must find someone like a tactful Libran who likes to be led, or someone so strong he will laugh at her and go on his own way — perhaps an Aries. She is so attractive and dynamic, she should have a happy marriage. But she won't change her spots — I know Chris.

I have another client and long-time friend who has learned that happiness doesn't always mean getting your own way. I have watched Sue go through one tragic affair and now she is faced with a situation not unlike that of Chris — the man she loves and who loves her can't — or won't — divorce. He is a Catholic and afraid if he divorced he might lose his children.

They tried to separate and both were so unhappy they couldn't do it. Now they are back together and she has accepted him on his terms. Meanwhile, she keeps open for the time when she might meet a man who feels as she does, wanting marriage and a family. Through astrology, she has learned how to compromise. So when and if such a man comes along, Sue is free to leave Harry. He also knows he is taking a chance on losing her because he won't divorce his wife.

Sue is no wimp! She has a fine brain, and uses it in her public relations firm. She is also so attractive she can't go into a supermarket without some man offering to carry her groceries home. She has Venus, the planet of beauty, joined to Neptune on the spiritual plane, both in the charming sign of Libra. And she has the fun-loving Sagittarius rising sign. Harry, her lover, also has Sagittarius rising, which explains the attraction. The same ascendant is not seen in charts very often and only those who share it know how special it is. In addition, they share the same position of Mars, the planet of sexual attraction. They both belong to the sentimental and romantic Pisces age which is slipping away. They fit so well I can't help hoping Harry will change his mind before another man appears.

What happens when I see trouble ahead for a couple very much in love? This happened to a couple of whom I was fond. Pam was a darling and she was in love with her boss, an outgoing and very popular man who had his own radio program in which he blended humor and information. I never missed it. In addition, he was in demand for personal appearances all over the country.

When he was at Columbia University giving a speech, an undergraduate in the audience — a saucy blonde — asked so many acute questions, he told her he wanted to talk to her after the lecture. That was Pam and she went to work for him as a Girl Friday when she graduated.

Dave had an office in the Wrigley Building and every Friday night he and Pam would have drinks and dinner in the Cape Cod Room at the Drake Hotel. My husband and I joined them a few times, then it became a regular occasion. He was a double Leo with his moon in Sagittarius and Pam had Sagittarius rising. He was older than she by twenty years, so at the start he treated her as a bright child.

Dave had been divorced for many years. He had a wife who hated him and two children who had been taught to loathe their father. He had never remarried. Burdened by heavy alimony, he also enjoyed being free of what had been a contentious marriage. But he let himself delight in Pam's quick mind and sense of fun that was like his. First, they were friends and then they fell in love.

Both were shy about getting themselves into a romantic relationship, but they couldn't avoid it. The attraction was too strong. "It was karma," I told Pam when she came to me for help.

I happened, happily, to be aware of what was happening almost before they were. Then they couldn't keep their secret and we were delighted. I never knew a man who had as many friends as Dave. Everybody was his pal, from the doorman to the cop on the beat. His genuine charm and kindness even won over Pam's family who worried about her marrying an older man. He planned to arrange for someone to take over his business for three months so they could take a trip around the world and have the captain of the ship marry them. They were both so excited and Dave seemed like a kid again.

Then destiny stepped in. I sensed that Pam was worried about him. He was working feverishly, trying to contact all of the stations airing his syndicated show and arrange for a suitable substitute. One night when he was supposed to join us at the Cape Cod Room, he never came. We took Pam home and a few days afterward she called and said he had gone to another restaurant and had waited there for hours.

"Something odd is happening," she told me. I had already seen trouble in both their charts, but didn't want to spoil their happiness. Soon she came and told me the doctors feared he was suffering from a neurological disease. He tried to work but it was hopeless. She was afraid to let him travel alone because he would get off at the wrong stop and call her at the office, bewildered because nobody had met him.

Eventually, he had to be put in a nursing home. He gave her power of attorney and she tried to take over his work, but she was a young girl dealing in a very tough world. Between visiting Dave at the nursing home and trying to run the business, Pam was nearing a breakdown herself. Finally her parents came west. They helped her sell the business and wanted to take her east with them for a rest. But she resisted. While he was alive, she went to see him every day, even when he no longer knew her. Only after he died did she go away for a much-needed rest. During her period of mourning, I could see there would be happy years ahead, and now she is engaged to be married to a wonderful man who adores her.

Many professional women today are not leaping into marriage. They want to test a relationship, see if it works before they commit themselves. Sometimes they learn enough to know they don't match. And sometimes they stop trying to find a man they want to marry and decide to have a child on their own, be a single mother á là *Murphy Brown*. When the popular TV series, *Cheers*, ended, the couple played by Shelly Long and Ted Danson decided to marry after having known each other for eleven years. Then, at the last minute, each one separately decided the relationship wasn't right, so they parted. And it happens similarly in real life.

There are two crises in every relationship, one at twelve years, the Jupiter cycle, and an earlier one at seven years. Remember the movie, *The Seven Year Itch*? Usually what happens around that time either ends or strengthens the relationship. Sometimes the early sexual excitement abates into something stronger and deeper. Or the birth of a child makes the difference, as it did with Woody and Mia. Or it's the end as it was for Chris and Jason. The next crisis occurs in five or six years for those who survive the first seven.

In the case of Mia and Woody, they split because, despite counseling, they were both so frozen emotionally that they could not open up and give warmth to each other. This applies to so many couples. With Chris's lover, Jason, his first marriage had so scarred him that he still carried the emotional hurt and could not open himself to another possible injury. She, instead of nurturing him, showing how little he had to fear, could not resist telling him what to do, aiming to re-shape him into an image of what she wanted in a husband.

Lack of confidence and self-esteem can also have their roots in early life. When a girl feels unwanted by her parents, it can lead to promiscuity. She jumps into any kind of love she can find. Boys who feel unwanted tend to crave love and attention so intensely they can never get enough love as they mature. Or they cling to what represents a family to a point of disaster — as did poor Allen who killed his sister's boyfriend. The other side of the coin is the parent, usually the mother, who cannot, will not, give up her child — again, usually a boy.

Let me tell you about Diane, a charming Aries, who was a broker at a prestigious Wall Street firm in New York. Tall and lovely, a natural clothes horse, she also was brilliantly successful. She commuted regularly on an express bus, as did a handsome young Capricorn lawyer employed by a prominent law firm. He asked her to lunch, and the romance went on from there. There was only one difficulty — she was a Protestant, and his relatives were strict Orthodox Jews. He was more liberal than his parents, but when after four years they decided to get married, religious differences presented a problem. Arnold finally defied his horrified mother and told her he was marrying Diane. The idea of his marrying a gentile was especially repugnant to his mother because he was the younger of her four children and the only boy.

Diane's mother, a cool Virgo, a top ad woman whose lawyer husband had died recently of cancer, agreed to help them arrange a civil service. Arnold sold his downtown condo and bought one on the Upper East Side, in a high-rise overlooking the East River, with a spectacular view. They wanted to get married at twilight and hold the reception in the condo. It took a lot of doing. Diane's mother found the judge and the two young people worked together to get the apartment in perfect shape, spending a great deal of money, most of it his, with decorating help from Diane's mother.

Meanwhile, the couple moved into Diane's rental apartment in Murray Hill. The preparations lasted nearly nine months. Engraved invitations had already been sent out when Diane called her mother, "I can't go through with it. I don't want to be tied to Arnold the rest of my life."

It turned out that Arnold, once a passionate lover, had become virtually impotent after he moved into Diane's apartment. Frantic, he consulted doctors and quacks. She was patient and tried to help but that only made him worse. The real problem was guilt because he knew he was breaking his mother's heart by marrying a gentile. Afterward, his mother told Diane, "I admire you so much for making the right decision. You and he never would have been happy."

Often the need of a woman to cling to a child, particularly a male child, is again due to the changing pattern of family life. We see more and more one-parent families headed by hard-working mothers. Often they sacrifice their lives for their child, or children. So it is hard for them to give up the ties. When an adult son or daughter, who is still a child to her, decides to leave her and get married, it is a bitter pill to swallow. Instead of welcoming the freedom to live her own life, she can never release her children.

Sometimes the children are able to pull away but it is difficult. These strong mothers, often Capricornians or Cancerians, are usually wonderful, admirable women who have struggled against odds, a neglectful or weak, abusive husband, so it is hard to give up the reins when children are grown and become adults. Women seem more adroit about escaping these clinging ropes of mother love than men because they are women born of women and understand the game. Men are too burdened by guilt — "after all, who gave birth to you?" Or the old adage, "A daughter's a daughter all her life. A son's a son until he takes a wife."

I grant you some mothers are right about apprehensions. Too many girls marry because they are tired of boring jobs and want the security of a man — preferably a successful man with money — taking care of them. My dentist's nurse, a pretty redhead, once asked me when he was out of the room, "How do I find a husband?"

I was rather staggered. Then, because her dentist boss is far from inexpensive, I suggested, "He must have a lot of attractive (i.e. rich) men patients." She answered petulantly, "They're either married or gay."

Men make the same mistake. The sex is so great they don't want to think of some other man enjoying *it* with *their* woman. Or, they need some one to take care of them the way *Mom* did.

And there is the attractive divorcee with two children who said to me, of a certain man she was dating. "Why shouldn't he marry me? He is a wonderful father to his kids and he would be good to mine. He's handsome and successful." I shocked her by asking, "What can you do for him?"

The willingness to bend (but not break), to give of oneself, is disappearing in this new world of women. So many not only want equality, they demand it, *they think they deserve it*. The militancy has worked. Women have, as the slogan goes, come a long way. But they are still often bewildered, vaguely aware of something gone wrong. It is significant that one slim book, *The Bridges of Madison County*, was recently the number one book of all best-seller lists for week after week.

It is a love story — a bittersweet love tale, some say, others insist it is soppy — of a married woman with a family who, in a short interval when her husband and children are away, experiences a perfect love affair with a stranger, a photographer passing through. The affair has to end, reality takes over, but the memory warms her otherwise prosaic life. It's not soap opera — modern soaps are full of bitter divorces — it is an old-fashioned love story. Recently, a client came in with the book in a pretty paper jacket she had made herself — and she's no teenager, she has a very responsible job.

Marriage and relationships are unsatisfactory — and failing — in so many cases today because today's busy women lack what we can only call intuition, the ability to recognize a need, perhaps a deficiency in the men they have chosen. They lack the understanding to sense that need and the flexibility to deal with it without alienating the man and destroying the marriage or relationship.

A client recently told me about her daughter, thirty-five, a talented Aries with two children, nine and twelve. She divorced her husband because he resented her success, was jealous of it. "I don't have time to waste on a man I've outgrown in every way."

True, he was making far less money than she did.

He was a salesman for a large company, by no means a flop. He got along with both bosses and clients because he was an easy-going Leo. He was hurt when Donna never went to his company's parties where wives were invited. He'd buy one of the kids a present and Donna would come home with something much grander and more expensive. His pride was hurt and he began staying out late at night, coming home drunk, forgetting anniversaries. The divorce gave her custody of the kids.

Her mother, a long-time client of mine, said to me, "Donna is missing something. She runs a successful business and is devoted to the children but she didn't understand intuitively what she was doing to Jack. I could see this coming a long time ago. They were so in love when they married but as time went on, without either of them knowing it, they were both changing, maturing. In her case, besides her obvious artistic talents, she was developing a feel for business and marketing her designs. But she was shoving her Leo husband off center stage. He was too proud to show his hurt and she was too self-centered to know what she was doing to him. So they split — and she is looking for a stepfather to her children."

This is the point I am trying to make with my clients who come to me with unhappy marriages, trying to help them through astrology to understand the men or women with whom they are involved. In days past, women's intuition saved many a marriage. A woman — working or not — was not so obsessed with success and need for self-expression that she forgot the needs of her husband.

Then there is Lorraine who was determined, from the time she was small, to become a writer. She wouldn't take typing or teaching courses, she was so afraid of being sidetracked, for in those days, it was still a man-dominated world. Pursuing her goal, she moved from Chicago to New York and got a job as a copywriter at a new advertising agency that was gaining a reputation for unusual and amusing work.

Her boss, who had founded the agency, was an ambitious Capricorn with Scorpio rising. Lured by his magnetism, every woman in the office was in love with him — but not Lorraine. She did her job brilliantly and always left the office at five o'clock, not waiting around, as some other girls did, hoping Ned would offer a cocktail invitation. Which he often did!

Of course, that was a challenge. Soon he began dropping into her office in the early afternoon to ask her to join him for drinks. Twice she had something else to do, but then she said yes. And that was the beginning of a secret romance, for he didn't want anyone in the office — particularly his secretary — to suspect he was courting her.

Lorraine was born on the cusp between Virgo and Libra. Cusp people often are unusual, and talented — she has Leo rising and an Aquarian moon. And he also had an Aquarian moon. This means an intellectual rapport which never failed to challenge and stimulate them both. He actually adored her. And their marriage — a surprise to many people — was a combination of sexual delight and excitement.

He didn't want her to continue working in his office, so he found her an agent, a top one, who encouraged her talent for fiction. One year, writing young love stories that were currently in demand in magazines, she earned more than he did — and he boasted about it. Instead of asking clients or employees out for drinks, he brought them home — men and women — so she would be entertained.

In the course of the work, she got fed-up with young love stories and began doing articles which entailed travel. He continued to be proud of her. But more and more, the people from the office he brought home were women. Ned was a long-time liberal and among the first to hire women in executive positions, paying them well. He was attracted to these women and proud of them. But that was all — Lorraine hoped. She welcomed them to their cocktail parties and, when she was away, he made no secret of the fact that he had dinner dates with them. His very openness was disarming.

Once when she was away on an assignment, she hurried to be home on Friday night — and found he was out. It was well after midnight when he came home. She was upset when he explained he had promised to take his art director out for her birthday and hadn't realized Lorraine would be home so early. The next day, he brought his wife roses as an apology. She let it go and said to herself *that was Ned*. She was the one he married, not the girls he took out for drinks. So life went on.

In April, to celebrate their twelfth wedding anniversary (remember the Jupiter cycle) they went to England on the QE2. It was rough and many passengers were sea-sick, including Ned. Lorraine was a good sailor and loved the tumult. Instead of staying in their cabin and watching Ned be sick, she stayed in the public rooms and didn't miss a meal. Neither did a British publisher whose wife was back in England. The two good sailors walked the decks together, shared meals, and talked about books and writing. Once when they were standing outside on the windswept deck, he put his arm around her and kissed her. She responded and they had a mini shipboard romance which they both recognized as just that.

When the storm was over, shaken passengers emerged, Ned among them. She welcomed him without guilt. She hadn't been taking revenge for his *petite amours* — at least she didn't think so. But on the last night, when they were all in the lounge having a farewell drink, the British publisher came over to say goodbye. He shook hands with Ned and kissed her.

When they went down to their cabin, Ned turned on her, "What the hell went on between you two lovebirds when I was down here so sick I couldn't lift my head?"

She tried to explain. He wouldn't listen. He sulked all the way to London and after they were ensconced at Claridge's. He didn't speak to her during dinner but afterward his love-making was frantic. Next day he was silent again. She said to him, "We didn't come all this way and spend all this money to have a silent honeymoon, did we?" Then it came out. He was ravingly, bitterly jealous. The fact that the British publisher had kissed her goodbye — what else had gone on?

She looked at him, more amazed than angry. She almost said, "What about your girls you bring home from the office? What about the night I came home early from a story and you forgot I was due and were out giving a birthday dinner for your art director?" Instead she recognized how much he cared for her and how afraid he was of losing her. She apologized and after that she never did anything that might threaten him. And they lived happily ever after until he died young of a heart attack.

When I tell this story to clients who are busy getting revenge on lovers for presumed infidelities, they look at me with astonishment. "That woman was an idiot. She had a perfect right to get even with him. He was a philanderer," and on and on. My only answer is, "She knew her man."

Let me show you how astrology helped me. I was slowly recuperating from a serious operation. One day I felt free from pain and well enough to put on lipstick, anticipating a good visit with my husband. When he came to the hospital, he stayed only a short time. I was both disappointed and hurt. Then I thought about his chart and studied it.

It was obvious he was going through some kind of a crisis that stressed his nervous system, and he was worried about his business. He didn't want to tell me because I wasn't well. So I changed my attitude from feeling sorry for myself and projected as positive and understanding an attitude as I could. Afterward, he told me how much he appreciated my understanding when he was undergoing a very difficult business decision. That strengthened our communication and intimacy. He never knew how hurt I had been, and how I had used astrology to give me the answers.

I recently attended the wedding of a niece. She is a doctor marrying another young doctor. One of the good things which has come out of the new freedom of women is the two-career family. Working together, they also grow together with the same interests and challenges. Sometimes, as in the case of two young brokers I know, they both lead a frantic pace, with personal trainers and business entertaining sandwiched between jobs. Their first crisis may come when they decide to have a family — or if one of them gets fired.

There are plenty of people trying to offer help to confused men and women who don't know where to turn. Countless books have been published, some helpful, but some actually harmful, distorting solutions. Of course, psychologists and analysts can help. But they don't find answers swiftly, when they are needed in a crisis. And their services are costly and can go on a long time.

And there is one problem with using psychologists and analysts. If we are seeking help trying to resolve a relationship, the psychologist or analyst can only understand our side of the relationship. And what he/she can learn about the other person involved is only what we see, which is, of course, biased. In astrology, we can look at the charts of both people and compare them.

I know many psychologists who use astrology very successfully in their work. Some won't admit it, for fear of offending their colleagues. But in this changing and turbulent world, barriers are dropping everywhere and even cynics are coming to appreciate the insight and understanding that planetary influences can bring to both the patient and therapist. As medical science is beginning to open up to the efficacy of Eastern methods and blending them with Western methods, so the philosophy and once-considered *occult* theories of the East are beginning to be tested and experimented with by the more conventional thinkers.

To achieve the intimacy which is essential in a relationship, we must communicate, and to communicate we must understand the nature of the other person and, above all, know ourselves. You *may* think you see. But ask yourself this: How many times do I realize how stubborn I am? Or how judgmental? How many times do I interrupt when someone I care about is telling me about something which upsets and worries him/her? Or, if you recognize this impatience in yourself, do you know why you do it? Or, do you simply say, "That's the way I am," with no thought of changing? That is the beginning of trouble, because if you don't wonder why you are acting the way you do, and are not thinking of how it affects him/her, there is a wall going up between you, and gradually the passion you felt for each other breaks down and the sexual attraction which was so exciting disappears — or turns to anger.

We must know each other intellectually, emotionally (that is, sexually). And the key to intimacy is communication. We must get through to the other person. And to do that, we not only must understand his/her nature, we must know ourselves. This is where astrology can help.

When I am comparing two charts, many elements come into the conclusion — not only the position of the sun at birth, but also the sign rising over the horizon at birth — called the ascendant — and the sign the moon is in. Actually, we must consider several hundred factors! If I can't see or talk to the client directly, I will ask to see a picture, for physical characteristics are connected to the different signs and planets. Then I calculate a chart — a road map — for the client to guide him/her in the course of his/her life.

Each one of us has certain characteristics that will attract the person with whom we want to share our lives. But this will happen not when we *think* we are ready but when the time is *right*. Perhaps we have to endure a tragedy or a trauma to deepen our understanding and growth. When we have learned from that experience and have accepted it without complaint, everything falls into place. We are changed in important ways, for the better, and open for the new adventure.

JUST FOR THE FUN OF IT –
A WORD ABOUT SUN SIGNS
The Twelve Zodiac Signs

This book was written to show the layman what real astrology is, how it can help guide our lives. Here I want to say a word of caution about relying too much on sun signs. What the astrologer refers to as "Sun Signs" are the twelve zodiac signs in which the sun is placed in each of the twelve months of the year. We do find certain characteristics are shared by people born in each month, but we must always keep in mind the fact that there are over seventeen hundred factors to be considered in each individual case. A person's *true* horoscope is a pattern — or chart — of the exact positions of each the eight planets — Venus, Mars, Saturn, Mercury, Jupiter, Uranus, Neptune, Pluto — and the sun and the moon *PLUS* hundreds of factors which relate to the electro-magnetic fields affecting that individual as a baby when he or she draws his or her first breath, and *for the rest of that person's life*!

Your *sign* only tells you what zodiac sign the sun was in when you were born. It is all very well to read your daily "horoscope" in the newspaper for fun — but don't take it out of context of your personal horoscope! Your true horoscope is a pattern — or chart — of the exact positions of each of the ten planets and hundreds of factors which relate to the electro-magnetic fields affecting you as a baby when you draw your first breath and for the rest of your life.

There are a number of mistaken clichés about which planets and signs combine to make a good marriage. A client came to see me in despair because she, a Cancerian, was seeing a man who had his sun in Gemini — "and my girlfriend says Geminis and Cancers are like oil and water."

I assured her that such generalizations are often nonsense. If you happen to have a friend who is a source of these clichés, ignore him/her. Actually, one of the best astrological combinations often lies in two neighboring signs. That's because Venus, the planet of love, is very likely to be in the sign just before or after yours. In this case, the man had his Venus on her sun in Cancer, and they were ideally suited as lovers. I told her that I would have to do his chart completely to be able to tell her if this would be any more than a passing affair.

But I have seen neighboring signs as a good omen in many cases. For example, Paul Newman (sun in Aquarius and moon in Pisces) and his wife Joanne Woodward (sun in Pisces and moon in Aquarius) have a marriage famous for the compatibility of two talented people. Or, Marlo Thomas and Phil Donahue — Marlo has her sun in Scorpio and the moon in Cancer while her north node of the moon is in Sagittarius, which is Phil's sun sign. The north node represents destiny and tells us that they were probably together in a previous life.

I know that sounds complex, but it really isn't. There is another basic clue: the position of the sun or moon on the other person's Venus, or on Mars. Before you listen to a well-meaning friend, consult an astrologer who knows what astrology is all about.

Let's look at the astrological reasons behind the close relationship of Burt Reynolds and Dinah Shore. I was reminded of this romance when I heard he had gone into a hospital for observation after her death.

She was nineteen years older than he. I hear clients question a relationship where the woman is much older than the man. Often I find out she has her Venus in the same sign as the man's sun. The attraction is inevitable. And when the man has Mars, the sex planet, on her sun, she responds to his magnitism. So the attraction is magical.

This was the situation with Burt and Dinah. Sensitive and talented Dinah had Venus in Aquarius on his sun while he had Mars in Pisces on her sun. With her Mars in Pisces on his Saturn, he caused her some hurt and disappointments but the tie of destiny is special. Of course, with his sun in Aquarius and moon in Libra, he loves women and will always have them in his life. But Dinah was unique. Burt also had Saturn, destiny, on her sun in Pisces, suggesting he would outlive her, which is what happened.

Sometimes the world is cynical when an older man marries a woman much younger. People say the attraction is her body or that he is trying to recapture youth before it is too late. But this is not necessarily so. Lauren Bacall was twenty-five years younger than Humphrey Bogart when they appeared together in a film. He was an established star, an intelligent, man's man who was very attractive to women. And, young as she was, she already had a strong personal style and an impressive background. This was true love. He had Mars, the planet of energy and sex, squaring (a ninety degree aspect) her Venus. Just as Bacall said in their first movie, "If you want me, just whistle," so astrologers whistle when they see this combination in a chart.

Mars is such a potent force both in sex and in war that sometimes it produces quarrels that find their way into the bedroom — a situation that can produce a couple who can't live together yet can't live without each other. I found myself in just such a situation when my husband and I fell in love. We were mad about each other but we also had wild quarrels. I knew why and we learned to make the planets work for us in a beautiful marriage that could have been a battlefield. There were strong Mars connections between our charts and Mars' energy is exciting and sexy — but could also stimulate arguments.

Jesus had his twelve disciples, the jury serving in the courts has twelve men, the idea being that each of the twelve signs of the zodiac should be represented: i.e., the twelve basic types of human nature — twelve different points of view! Let's start with Aries.

ARIES – March 21- April 20

Energy! Vitality! Action! Enthusiasm! Impatient! Quick! Aries is the leader. In front of the crowd! Bossy, opinionated, venturesome. Not afraid of anything — no one and nothing — least of all, what others think. Arians get things started for others to finish. Cannot follow. Impatient, they get results NOW or try something else! Sometimes contrary and argumentative. Prone to headaches, they give them to others — need to slow down and give others a chance.

Things are never dull when Aries appears — how would things get started without them? Always breaking new ground, to the point and with authority, they may not always be right, but they're never in doubt.

Never happy unless at the helm, perfect for a talk show host, their physique tells the story: strong body, not heavy, longish face, pointed angular features, prominent ears, longish nose, and flashing eyes — laughing one minute, shooting sparks the next, usually brilliant blue. Quick to move and quick to speak — nothing is fast enough. Loves competition, knows he/she will win. *Never slows down, never grows old!* Debbie Reynolds shows us this.

The Aries woman goes after her man — gets him *soon*, or goes after another. Aries is competitive, has to be *first* in everything. Man or woman, Aries never lies. Is very direct, following the straight line. May run over you if you get in the way. Must have the last word. *Ain't afraid of nothin'!* Loves a good scrap. Sometimes too aggressive, stepping on the toes of more sensitive souls. A touch of arrogance, may come on too strong.

192

Many changes are taking place — some exciting and happy, some disturbing and upsetting at the time, but setting the stage for the future! Patience is required during these next few years.

Talk show host David Letterman is an Aries! Conan O'Brian, another talk show host, with his enthusiasm, his red hair and sharply pointed nose asks penetrating questions with disarming candor, is frankly competitive but not jealous. Other Aries — Henry Kissinger, Marlon Brando, Queen Elizabeth II, Vincent van Gogh, Tennessee Williams, Wilbur Wright.

TAURUS – April 21- May 20

Lovable and loving! Deliberate, thoughtful, cautious. Loyal, stubborn, thorough. The bull cannot think fast, so how can he/she act fast? Nor can Taureans accept ideas they can't understand. Creative, yet methodical. Artists, musicians, actors. They must *feel* their way in everything they do — in love, sex, food. *Terrific* chefs. Never try to change the mind of the bull, never try to persuade or argue. It's no use. Set an example for the bull to follow, but don't *PUSH*. The Taurean will stand still — or worse, back up.

Taurus is a lover, not a fighter. Unless forced into a fight, and then he/she can land a punch one will never forget! Like everything else Taurus does — making love, preparing dinner, acting on stage, or using the voice. In fact, Taurus is known for his/her voice — Barbara Streisand, Bing Crosby, Perry Como, Carol Burnett — and its sexiness — Cher.

Never try to *sell* an idea — show him/her *how*, not *why*. There is depth of feeling behind everything the bull does. Leave your house plants with your Taurus friend when you go away — they will be happy under his/her care, and so will your pets. But the pets may not want to leave when you return!

Slow to start, but never gives up — even when he/she should. *Never forgets, never forgives!* A promise made is a promise kept. The bull is deeply serious, but has an earthy sense of humor — sexy, sometimes vulgar. *Taureans love to eat* and have rounded features, thick hair, and eyelashes. The bulls walk with their weight on the heels, as though someone might try to pull the ground out from under them, a threat to their security.

Possessive of their loved ones and possessive of

material things, Taureans must learn to let go, but only rejection will teach them — you can't! Devoted and loyal by nature, Taurus is inclined to *hold on* too long — if Taureans finally let go, they never change back.

Taureans like physical contact with people. They have a touching quality about them. Note talk show host Jay Leno of the *Tonight Show* who often touches his favorite guests, not in a sense of intimacy, but just because he likes them.

Taurus can never get enough love (or sex) or *anything* — and moderation must be cultivated, lest over-indulgence destroy the beauty and the talents which abound — Orson Welles!

Taurus has staying power, holds the fort, so to speak, defends the home. Taurus has a strong voice, or special resonance. A strong build, resistance. And a strong capacity for love. Not always communicative, but emotions run deep. Just don't let Taureans swallow you up! Taurus is non-aggressive, but is patient and reliable. Slow to anger, but if and when *really* provoked, *WATCH OUT*! Taurus is called an "earth" sign, and if you feel a tremor, *LEAVE* at once, before the earth *QUAKES*! In other words, before the anger builds and explodes. Candice Bergen and Shirley MacLaine are lovable but *STRONG*. And how about adorable Shirley Temple Black, now a symbol of conservatism?

GEMINI – May 21- June 21

The twins of the zodiac — two people in one, sometimes three!

Many Geminis make big careers with talk, talk, talk! If you want to say something to a Gemini, listen for a comma and jump in right away. Wait too long and there's no comma! The communicators of the zodiac, they are so eager to report the latest, they interrupt every minute. Talented in many areas, they must learn to focus on one at a time to avoid scattering their versatile energies. The artist, the scientist, the psychologist. Most always intellectual, though occasionally superficial. And always unpredictable: first one, then the other.

Possessed of (and perhaps by) a highly sensitive nervous system. Always thinking — many thoughts at once — changing from one to the other. Everything comes into Geminis' lives in doubles. Two loves at a time, two careers, and all in extremes. No wonder they are restless and nervous! They are happier when juggling two things at a time. Too much discipline throws off their rhythm. They need to play games for relief. A little flirtation here and there doesn't hurt — except the ones who love them. The rhythm kids in the zodiac, a sensitive touch, sensuous. Be flexible and adaptable and you'll find Geminis worth the trouble!

At their best, they are flexible and adaptable — at their worst, they are impossible. To resist them is to miss a lot of fun — and to avoid a lot of trouble! Multi-talented and versatile, they have many attractions — at least two at a time. They see everything and everyone, so their twinkling eyes are constantly moving, changing from one to the other while their toes are tapping out a tune. Beautiful hands and legs. They see everything around them and find humor in it all!

P.S. Wouldn't you know, vivacious talk show hosts Joan Rivers and Jenny Jones are both Gemini. Marilyn Monroe was a Gemini — so, too, John F. Kennedy. Other Geminis such as Stephanie "Steffi" Graf, Joe Montana, and Frank Lloyd Wright have been considered people of many personalities. Look at the great Judy Garland.

Very often you may know some one who has all of these characteristics, but was born under a different sign. The person probably has the moon or the ascendant in Gemini. Remember, these two — the moon and the ascendant (or rising sign at time of birth) will provide some of the traits that are not found in the sun sign. Confusing? Yes, but true. Gemini includes some of the most talented and versatile people in the zodiac. The list goes on and on — Lawrence Olivier, John Wayne, Paul McCartney —.

CANCER – June 22- July 22

Imagination! The most sensitive sign in the zodiac. Sensitive to the mental atmosphere in the environment, to the reactions of others, to nature, to animals, to color. Several of the French impressionist artists were Cancerians. Should follow a profession which uses sensitivity and imagination. Either the arts or psychology, medicine, counseling, writing, teaching. The sensitivity *must* be used in a positive way — dealing with others or in self expression — lest it take the negative route and result in moods and hurt feelings. Cancer will take offense when none is intended. Intuitive and kind, Cancerians wouldn't hurt a fly, but they'll *never* forget a slight or offense, and some day will *get even*. Tenacious and persevering, Cancer is the survivor. Cancerians take longer to gain self confidence, but they last longer.

The Cancer woman is often full-breasted — *or* flat. She's very feminine and protective of her men and needs to learn to let go. Circuitous in conversation, touching all the details in a story — serious and thoughtful, but usually blessed with a sense of humor. Like Phyllis Diller! As parents, Cancerians can be *too* caring!

Talk show host, Geraldo Rivera, is a typical Cancerian. Known for his far-out guests, he looks for the fantastic — that is imagination and curiosity. The unusual appeals to these Cancerians. They're very emotional and easily hurt. On the defensive, they try to protect themselves and those they care about.

Other well-known Cancerians: Princess Diana, Andrew Wyeth, Peter Paul Rubens, Louis "Satchmo" Armstrong, Rembrandt Harmensz van Rijn, John D. Rockefeller, Arthur Ashe. Dynamic Merv Griffin is one.

LEO – July 23- August 22

The Kings — or Queens of the jungle, and don't you forget it! Stroke them admiringly, and they'll purr. Ignore them, and you'll pay for the slight one way or another, but you won't even know why! Give them center stage, *after all they deserve it!* Aren't they the best? Actors? The center of their world (and yours), they do *everything* with *style.* And, by the way, they strut or prance; they actually present themselves! How about multi-talented Tony Bennett?

Born with a sense of the dramatic, they also do *everything* with *flair.* The head of a conservative banking house startles his employees at early morning meetings when he appears in a bright yellow or scarlet tie. This Leo has a stand-up desk so he will never have to look up to anyone! (After all, the lions are not very tall as a rule). But they have big hearts, and cannot bear to appear small, in any way. Sometimes they may be so in need of being the star that the very audience they wish to impress may resent them, and they'll never know it.

Proud of a thick mane of hair, growing from a widows's peak or an irregular hairline (like the lion's) with deep-set eyes, square shoulders, deep chest, and long torso, the lion will often exaggerate his situation without realizing it. Perfectly sincere, he believes his own publicity!

Lest our Leo friends take offense at all this, we must compliment them on their innate talents: the style with which they express themselves, the generous spirit which tinges every gesture. When they love, it is with all their being; when they give a gift, it has to be the *very best* they can find.

Leo is the sign of the theater, and of teaching, and of children. Jacqueline Kennedy Onassis was a Leo. Keep this in mind, and you can't fail to appreciate what they bring to the rest of us! A Leo mother may criticize her cubs, but God forbid someone else does!

Some of my favorite people are those lovable lions. Other famous Leos — Bill Clinton, Napoleon Bonaparte, Judge Lance Ito, Robert Redford, Earvin "Magic" Johnson, Dustin Hoffman, Orville Wright, Henry Ford, George Bernard Shaw, George Shearing, Kathie Lee Gifford, Regis Philbin (Leo/Virgo cusp).

VIRGO – August 23- September 22

The critic. The analyst. The expert. Always thinking. Observes every detail and overlooks nothing. The detective, the doctor, actress, writer, engineer, interior decorator. Neat! Immaculate! Discriminating! But perfectionism can limit the imagination, dull the spontaneity and lose the fun of fantasy. It also helps to make a brilliant student.

Never try to fool a Virgo. *Keep your word, be there on time!* Virgo will appreciate you, but insists you do things right. Show you care and don't flub or the Virgo will lose respect and may be too critical, which can spoil a friendship.

Sometimes it may seem as though Virgo is not responsive, when actually he/she is taking it all in. Virgos consider every detail and plan what they will do. It isn't that they don't feel, but rather they have gone beyond their feelings to the point where they are analyzing the effect upon you and the consequences!

The two main attorneys, Marsha Clarke (prosecution) and Robert Shapiro (defense), opposing each other in the O.J. Simpson murder trial are Virgos, with the moon in Gemini — brilliant! My friend, the psychologist Louis Brossard, Ph.D. is a Virgo. He says, "I generally rephrase what the person has said and ask him a question about it. . .and so he is confronted with what you get out of what he said, and of course you may get an instant denial, so you look at him in a dumbfounded way and say, 'I'm sorry I misunderstood. Can you explain it to me again in some way?' So he really has to be listening to what you are saying."

A bit tricky? No wonder Virgos make such clever

lawyers! — or talk show hosts such as TV's Regis Philbin, who has the moon in Virgo. Sexy? Of course — they know how and *when* to turn it on!

There are so many well known Virgos — Sophia Loren, Peter Falk, Lauren Bacall, Joan Lunden, Ingrid Bergman, J.P. Morgan, Bruce Springstein (Virgo/Libra cusp). Virgo is the master technician in the arts, whether acting, writing, or playing an instrument, such as pianist Bobby Short.

LIBRA – September 23- October 23

Libra needs a partner in life, but may not realize it. Romance, love and beauty are necessary to provide the balance without which Libra is incomplete. Blessed with a spontaneous charm and a beautiful smile which lights up the whole face, Librans are welcome wherever they go.

Known for their strategy, Librans consider both sides of a point of view, weighing and balancing one side against the other. "We must be fair!" Fine lawyers, diplomats, even generals, they are known for their fairness. General (and later President of the United States) Dwight D. Eisenhower was known for his consideration of the men who served under him, and for his ability to *think* of himself in his *enemy's place* (World War II and Hitler) — how his *enemy* would likely react to a given situation.

It takes a lot to anger a Libran, but if you do, you may as well throw in the towel; it's all over! All of a sudden!

Vulgarity, coarseness, and ugliness, Libra finds repulsive — especially in sex. Non-aggressive by nature, Libra wants you to make the decisions, to say what you want. Libra is happy when you are happy — especially when you are considerate and tactful. Meanwhile Libra may procrastinate or seem to — until he/she *feels sure about it!*

A positive-thinking partner to take the lead and make the final decision is the answer for a Libra. Two Librans together may never decide where or when to go for the evening, so they wind up not going anywhere! And if you are a Libran, you have had this experience more than once, until you learned to make the decision yourself — at last!

Decisive leaders in Aries are helpful, even when bossy — or a fixed Taurus or Leo — they'll *never* change their minds, so Libra won't have a chance to go back and forth over the decision.

Librans have to learn to make their own decisions! And so they may be placed in a situation (by fate, if you will) where they have to take a stand — like Mahatama Ghandi.

Libra is generally artistic, gracious, and charming, such as the actresses, Angela Lansbury and Suzanne Somers, and TV personality/reporter Barbara Walters. Other notable Libras — Jimmy Carter, John Lennon, T.S. Elliot, Martina Navaratilova.

SCORPIO – October 24- November 22

Scorpios are called the surgeons of the zodiac. They often make brilliant psychiatrists because they get to the heart of problems. Perceptive.

Known as the sex sign because of its intensity, Scorpio has a powerfully strong will and can control any situation if desired, either because he/she is simply not interested at the moment, or because he/she prefers the discipline. Magnetism is powerful and it can turn on — turn *you* on — or completely shut off suddenly, when the energy is directed into another channel of expression.

Scorpios are so intense they often seem self-centered. Pablo Picasso was a Scorpio and certainly deep into himself without much regard for anyone else. Or there's Richard Burton, whose life was centered on acting.

Mysterious! You will never *really know* a Scorpio. The Scorpio doesn't *really know* himself (or herself). A combination of the spiritual — the intuitive psyche — with the materialistic makes a rather subtle mysterious personality *not* understood by many and therefore misinterpreted. Considered secretive by others, Scorpio will not divulge your secrets as long as you trust him with the truth — however he/she will see through you if you don't tell the truth!

A wonderful friend — be sure you are worthy! Robert Dole is a Scorpio, as is Katharine Hepburn. Lee Strasburg, the famed drama coach, was another.

Scorpios always seem to hold something back when dealing with ordinary humans, for they want to pour everything into their acting or writing or painting, such as Georgia 0'Keeffe or Claude Monet. Note talk show interviewer Larry King who asks such perceptive questions.

Often dark-eyed, or with mysterious gray-green eyes, Scorpios are very attractive to the opposite sex. They often have deep-thrilling voices (again, Richard Burton) and work their way through a variety of love affairs without really committing to one. But when they do, it is with typical Scorpio intensity. They make wonderful surgeons for just this trait — when they operate, they don't hesitate, they go right to the source of the problem.

Because of their reticence and extreme independence, Scorpios are probably the least understood of all the signs of the zodiac. Scorpio is the detective of the zodiac, the sexy private eye who uncovers your secrets and reveals nothing of himself. Trust him, if he's/she's on your side — but not a word if he isn't!

If you love a Scorpio, don't intrude. Allow privacy. It can make him — or her value you above all others. When the Scorpion cares about you, you'll get his or her all. If the Scorpion doesn't care, forget it.

Some are materialistic, some are spiritual, mystics. The terrific electricity of the Scorpio is a powerful force for good when used constructively — a frightening source of evil if allowed to destroy! Currently, the intensity of Scorpio is demonstrated in the struggle between good and evil we see all around us, as the changes in our society take place, and we see a glimmer of the ultimate survival and triumph of good. That is the significance of the passing of the planet Pluto through Scorpio from September 1989 to November 1995.

So we have just one year more of the Pluto pressure which becomes more intense every day! Then we will experience a shift of energy, and we'll begin to emerge from the stagnant chaos of the present. Thank God!!

Other magnetic Scorpios — Hillary Rodham Clinton, Johnny Carson, Prince Charles, Robert Kennedy, Grace Kelly, Martin Luther, Dr. Jonas Salk, Julia Roberts, Bruce Jenner.

SAGITTARIUS – November 22- December 21

DON'T FENCE ME IN! The bachelor sign—men or women!

That's Sagittarius — the adventurous idealist who roams the world seeking perfection which cannot be found. Ever curious, fun-loving, active and athletic, Sagittarians make friends wherever they go — and they'll go anywhere — in the mind if not in the body. They "never saw a man they didn't like" — love everything that is open and free — perhaps too many! Spur-of-the-moment impulses, sincere and blunt in speech, calling things as they see them, yet they don't want to hurt.

They love animals, nature, and growing things, music and dancing. Should be around horses and should have their own. Or at least, play the horses and go to the track! Sometimes they actually look a little horsey — longish chin, devil within! Long legs, narrow hips, strong thighs, long stride. They think, but they don't think before they talk!

A new opportunity cycle opens up in 1995 or 1996, followed by the transition of Pluto from Scorpio into Sagittarius for a long cycle, which should be far happier than we have known for a long time. It will initiate new methods, new attitudes, new expectations. Hooray!!

Only the planet Pluto traveling through Sagittarius can see a rebirth of religious beliefs and a renewal of spiritual values, with idealism lifting up mankind and renewing the joy of living. Or, the transformation will take a long time, and require a real struggle, but some of us believe that it is possible, and that it *will* happen! Only the magical idealism of Sagittarius can bring it about!

Sagittarius is a sign of music: Frank Sinatra — with his beautiful phrasing. Hoagy Carmichael — still remembered for the phrasing of "Buttermilk Sky". (If you are too young to know the song, do some research through your Sagittarius musician friends!) Dionne Warwick is one.

Even though the sign the sun is in at birth can only give us some basic traits of an individual, with observation and reflection on our part, we can understand quite a lot about a particular person. Sometimes the sun sign will tell us more about the person than he(she) knows himself(herself)!

Sagittarius is constantly searching for the impossible dream — Don Quixote himself (or herself as the case may be)!

Some famous Sagittarians — Woody Allen, Winston Churchill, Mark Twain, Ludwig van Beethoven, and Walt Disney. Adventure is their middle name!

CAPRICORN – December 22- January 20

Ambition! Hard work and perseverance. The willingness to set the goal and proceed to attain that goal, step by step to the top. Give a Capricorn a job to do and consider it done! Capricorn plans far ahead and succeeds no matter how long it takes. Disappointment or loneliness in childhood teaches Capricorns to stand on their own — they learn early in life that it won't be easy, and so they seem ageless — older when young, and younger when they grow old.

Often a Capricorn-type woman (especially with the moon or ascendant in Capricorn) will marry a younger man, and help him to succeed. She has business ability, is an organizer no matter how feminine or ingenuous she may be. When married to an older man, she provides devotion and strength he can count on. Capricorn strives for results, one way or the other.

Successful in politics and business, Capricorns are the dynasty founders, the fortune builders. Many of the show biz celebrities — who start in childhood, carry the responsibility for their family, climb to the top, fall down and come back up again — have the moon in Capricorn to give the steel down deep within!

Sometimes they may seem cold or unemotional, but they need affection from others, even when they're undemonstrative. Capricorn has a longish chin, perhaps pointy, goat-like, and rather large eyes, very round, with the eyelid drooping over the outer corner. Sound funny? Observe it, and when you see it, never underestimate the will to succeed! Take a look at loveable George Burns, now in his nineties!

Although the other planetary positions in the chart will tell of the special talents, the Capricorn part of the nature will *make* him/her *work* to develop them!

There are countless celebrity Capricorns — Robert E. Lee, Janis Joplin, Richard Nixon, Benjamin Franklin, Howard Hughes, Martin Luther King, Jr., Humphrey Bogart, Edgar Allen Poe, Henri Matisse, Muhammad Ali (Cassius Clay) and on and on!

Capricorn is the organizer, the CEO. *And don't you forget it!* He/she must feel respected by those around him/her — especially family members — and the *corporation.*

Capricorns are very concerned with the opinion of those in authority — the boss, the public in general, and *Ms. Manners.* Is he or she doing the correct *thing*? Will others approve?

Money represents success. Possessions are a symbol of importance. Are they the *best*? Are they the *finest*? Do they *equal* those of the neighbors? Capricorn has the *desire* to be the *best* — but the other planetary positions at the moment of birth supply the *talents.* Study them carefully. Capricorn Mary Tyler Moore has Scorpio rising to give her that sexy quality. Every Capricorn will have *other* talents combined with the Capricorn traits.

__AQUARIUS__ – January 21- February 18

DIFFERENT! That's what we say about Aquarius, the individualist in the zodiac. He marches to a different drummer. Magnetic, original, Aquarians stand out from the crowd. And yet we find them dealing with groups, leading the public, teaching new ideas in some unusual way. Adored by others, yet not fully understood because of the detachment which enables them to take a perspective on the large picture, ever seeking the best for the largest number of people — the crowd, the group.

They may seem cold to more sensitive and emotional people who simply don't understand why they cannot feel close. How can there be real intimacy with the Aquarian who is involved with the universe? Actually, there is a strong spiritual nature internally though it may not always show the managerial and administrative talents which are so strong!

Aquarians stand out from the crowd because they are both impersonal and humanitarian. To others who are less sure of themselves and where they are going, the Aquarian may seem smug or distant, simply because he/she knows what he/she knows! A highly mental sign, Aquarians are sometimes restless and bored, always looking to the future. In search of new methods, they make the architects, the playwrights, the designers, and the teachers.

They're on a different plane. Abraham Lincoln and Franklin D. Roosevelt—they saw the large picture for America. Aquarians are not satisified with the status quo—but want accomplishments—life—to be better. They're the world's saviors—often rebels.

And so it is not surprising to learn that Oprah

Winfrey, who actually opened up the modern approach to talk shows, as she encourages the members of her audience to learn from their discussions with each other, is an Aquarian! She doesn't need outside guidance because her detached viewpoint combines with her deep-rooted spiritual concepts to provide the uniquely Aquarian perspective. The Aquarian draws from the past, and what is stored within, to build for the future. Their personal talents are unique—special for them. Notice Sonny Bono and Norman Mailer.

So many Aquarians are in the public eye — basketball star Michael Jordan, Chicago newspaper columnist Judy Markey, handsome Paul Newman! Notable others — Charles Lindbergh, Clark Gable, Jack Lemmon, Thomas Edison, Mikhail Baryshnikov, George Herman "Babe" Ruth.

 PISCES – February 19- March 20

Sensitive! Intuitive! Moody! — similar to Cancer — and sometimes dual — similar to Gemini. Some of the most talented of all musicians, dancers, actors, writers. Not always understood nor appreciated, due partly to their own negativity. Inclined to worry and self doubt, hesitant to show their emotions for fear of rejection, thus inviting the very disappointment they dread. Impressionable and vulnerable, they are happiest when they discover their own special talent (often hidden) and pursue it. This requires self-reliance, which strengthens in the middle years, after the experience of sorrow.

The year 1995 will continue a two-year Saturn cycle of growth, never easy, but the results can be amazing and inspiring! Regardless of their personal stage in life, Pisceans will find new meaning to their lives, and new reasons for being here. This is an excellent time for Pisceans to rediscover themselves, and their value to others.

The Pisces woman is very feminine, needs a leader to make decisions and give her confidence, but she does not respond well to harsh criticism or rude commands. This could cause moodiness or depression, loneliness. Yet she needs action to bring her into reality, tinged with romance! TLC is needed here. Perhaps this is why Piscean Elizabeth Taylor wanted to be married all of her adult life!

Once Pisceans learn to bring their dreams down to earth and put them to work, and once they stop swimming around in circles, their intuition and special talents will bring them a taste of fame and its rewards, as it is for Elizabeth Taylor and Liza Minnelli.

The Pisces man is sensuous but usually lacks self-assurance, inclined to worry too much about nothing! He must learn not to be influenced by everything others tell him. Pisces men are too clever to be so gullible!

Other famous Pisceans — Nat "King" Cole, Michelangelo Buonarroti, Pierre Auguste Renoir, Frédéric Chopin.

CYCLES

The seven-year cycles of life have been recognized and observed since time began. In fact, the seven-year cycles serve to measure time. It really is surprising that it seems only astrologers relate these cycles to two planets, Saturn and Uranus, in addition to the phases of the moon. Saturn is often called the Planet of Destiny, and Uranus the Planet of Change. Every seven years Uranus moves into the following sign of the zodiac, indicating different types of happenings and growth for each seven years, punctuated by the cycles of Saturn.

The aging process follows this schedule — every seven years we suddenly notice the marked change in ourselves and those around us — the change in fashions, in the tone of world events and human behavior. When Saturn squares Saturn (forming a ninety-degree aspect or angle to its natal place) at the age of seven, or a little beyond that, a person is fully incarnated. He/she is *here*, not just primitive. The human being has arrived.

That's why we find fathers taking more of an interest in their children as they grow up beyond seven and less interest in them as infants. Their mothers take care of them as infants, but by the time they are seven, they have already become human beings.

When they get to be about fourteen, and Saturn is opposing Saturn, that's when adolescence rears its ugly head and it's like a new birth. He/she is a different person — an adult human being coming to be. Now when he/she reaches the age of twenty-one or about that, the person approaches Uranus squaring Uranus. Rebellion! Nobody knows more about *everything* than twenty-one year olds! At the same time, they have the arrogance of immaturity. As they approach twenty-two, Saturn comes in and they have to take responsibility for all this freedom that they decided they must have.

By the time age twenty-nine arrives, Saturn returns to its natal place, and these people now have to give up all of their fantasies about what they were going to do and be and face the fact that this is adulthood, this is what they've done, and now they must take responsibility for their actions. They have to find some way to survive on their own for themselves. During this time, a person experiences the same squares (ninety-degree aspects between Saturn and planets).

When a person comes to the age of thirty-six he or she has Saturn squaring Saturn again with problems to live up to and get past. The person has to do what it is he or she actually needed to do at age twenty-nine if he or she didn't finish it — and most people don't finish it by then.

By age forty-two to forty-five — that's the time when marriages begin to break-up or a parent dies, or the last (or only) child is born, or a late marriage begins, or a new career — there are new beginnings, rebellion. Uranus opposed to Uranus. People say, "I have put up with this. I can't put up with it any more. It's too much for me." That's mid-life crisis time. Very soon afterward a person has a problem with Saturn.

If people go through this time without much change, the kinds of yokes that they didn't throw off at age forty-two to forty-five, they start throwing off at age sixty-three, as Uranus squares Uranus again (rebellion). Where the person had attempted to achieve his/her freedom from bondage at the age of forty-two to forty-five, he/she simply rises above it at the age of sixty-three. A person knows what he/she knows and he/she is not going to go on someone else's trip. One shouldn't fear the expectations of other people. At sixty-three one has enough maturity not to get into battles over it. There is a tendency to put other people in their places and exercise the freedom that is theirs.

Now Saturn continues on, but after the age of fifty-nine the second Saturn returns. Saturn has in a sense done its job and while there are some people who feel their Saturn aspects later in their sixties, generally they have the idea when they are fifty-nine (or thereabouts) that the world they have created for themselves is the world they have earned. If they don't have this attitude, there is little one can do for them. (Most people achieve success or make a wonderful move.)

Some spring forth, they know intuitively what they need to do at about age fifty-nine and it takes that arrogance at sixty-three — that squared Uranus — to actually do it. So if I know the age of a client, I have at least some idea of the kind of stage he/she is going through at the time.

A friend, age sixty-three, decided he should change girlfriends — the current one did not love him enough to divorce her husband! — and while he was driving to a tryst with the new one, he suffered an aneurysm and died. Perhaps we should not rebel and change our lives at sixty-three?!

The completion comes at the age of eighty-four

when people have, in a sense, gone the entire circle and they know all they're going to know. I see the age of eighty-four and the Uranus return as a kind of completion when many people opt out. That is a time that people often think something like, "I've gone through it, I know it all, I've done all this. 'Bye, see you later." Of course, there are a few wonderful exceptions — geniuses who produce their best in these years who seem to be ageless, and find new loves!

There's one place that the cycles don't work and that's at the ages between twenty-five and twenty-seven, when transiting Pluto joins the natal Neptune. I find that's a crazy time for a lot of people. It's true that many more people are more liberated in their ideas about marriage these days and they are more apt to be able to face the fact that some marriages serve their purpose and then come to an end.

There are many people these days who can face that reality so they can protect themselves from living in a dead marriage. By the same token, sadly, it does not always happen that two people in the married pair share that concept. Many women have a tendency to believe that they have been abandoned, but I have seen among my clients evidence that men feel frequently as abandoned as the women do. Some of the men are actually very broken-up by divorce and never get over it. It's not as clearly delineated as some people might think. The kind of ego that you see that is often associated with males is no longer exclusively a male "thing". There are women with male egos. Some women will no longer tolerate a relationship in which the man expects her future and her career to be secondary to his. They just will not sit still for it!

Meanwhile, Pluto in Scorpio is changing the sexual relationship between people completely.

There is no doubt about the fact that Pluto going through Scorpio is going to put the male/female, men and women kind of situation, in a new space. It's going to have to be renegotiated, because the attitudes of the past are not going to be appropriate. We are already finding the Plutonian transits affecting this and we will see it affected more with time.

In the late sixties and seventies I began to observe some of the planetary indications of the changes in sexual behavior with which we are now quite familiar. Whereas I used to recognize the homosexuals by the emphasis in their charts on the *secret* houses — the placement of the sexy planets in the sixth and twelfth sectors and the erotic influence of one planet upon another, used to be commonplace in the "gay" charts — suddenly these planets appeared in the *open* houses, the first house of self-expression, the eleventh house of friendships, the seventh house of partnership, etc. Then "gays" came out into the open, demanding recognition.

The attitudes toward each other in heterosexual relationships also appeared to be changing — a certain detachment, less emotional and loving connections, as though sex had less meaning on the personal level — more objective, searching for self-fulfillment and satisfaction, unwilling to give of oneself, to take a chance of being hurt, or to give to each other freely — afraid to love deeply.

It would seem the computer age may automatically eliminate the personal touch in interpersonal contacts. There is less personal interaction. More and more people are working at home, not in offices, communicating by computer. Even children who can barely write are playing games on their computers instead of with their playmates. And lovers use E-mail while lonesome souls seek companionship in computer groups. Today, every relationship is viewed as, "How do we relate to each other?" not, "How truly do we love each other?"

In the fall of 1993 we had the conjunction (joining) again of Uranus in Capricorn with Neptune, which we've been feeling for quite some time — the sudden and surprising upsets all around us, affecting civilization, weather, environment, human behavior, politics — all is change, and much of it shocking. But the changes we are seeing now, as we approach the Age of Aquarius, consist of bloodshed and violence. As Pluto goes into Sagittarius in 1995, we have another renaissance — one beyond our wildest imaginations as it results in tremendous innovations affecting communications and travel. We already have glimpses of the fascinating future!

Meanwhile, we have chaos, and horrible suffering. The homeless are sleeping in the streets, kids are murdering for kicks, and guns are standard equipment in our schools. Nature seems in the same mood of violence, giving us floods and earthquakes, tornados, and vicious weather ruining our crops. Abroad we have civil and tribal wars, and the murder of thousands of innocent civilians.

As an astrologer, I see what this is doing to people. The family, as a loving group, interacting with each other, is a rarity. Divorces are routine and there are so many children of divorce that private schools provide spaces in applications to list stepfathers.

When this planetary line-up happened one hundred seventy-one years ago, the Grand Alliance in Europe occurred, which was to bring peace about for the next thousand years. Now, instead of the Grand Alliance, we have the treaty negotiations. The fact is, we are going to be in a new space — and in just the same way that the Grand Alliance didn't work — because what it was meant to deal with had been changed almost beyond recognition by the time that particular conjunction in Capricorn had been completed — the negotiations or treaties will not work.

We're facing a long range trend here, too. The year 1492, when Pluto went into Scorpio (as it is now), was the beginning of The Renaissance. We are in a *new* renaissance — new kinds of communications are coming about, new kinds of worlds are being developed, both for nations and for people, and the relationships that are going to emerge in the future are going to be measurably different from those in the past.

We can see what happened to language during the last renaissance. What's happening now is that information is being completely transformed. Up until the present all scientific development had to base itself on preexisting scientific knowledge. People had to know certain facts, they had to go to school. They had to have a background in their own intelligence. With Pluto's transit through Scorpio this time, the *new* renaissance is going to be that when somebody wants something done, he/she has only to specify a command to machines and the machines will do the research.

The planet Pluto entered the sign Scorpio in November 1984. Scorpio is the sex sign, and Pluto is a catalyst. It penetrates the area it passes through, scraping the dregs so they can be recycled — or renewed — brought to the surface to be examined and analyzed, rebuilt, not destroyed or replaced. And this is what is happening now to SEX — and to morals, beliefs, and philosophies.

All hell is breaking loose! Crime in the streets — murder next door — copulation in public places. Where are we headed? Where is it leading us? How much longer can this continue? Conditions are now as never imagined before, even in society's most negative moments. It would seem crime can not get worse! Meanwhile, we have to go through a painful period of cleansing. First drugs must be cleaned out, as well as social diseases.

Scorpio is the sex sign and is penetrating the area as the planet Pluto passes through it, bringing poisons and corruptions of life to the surface, scraping the dregs so they can be examined before a period of cleansing begins. This means years of healing, spiritually and physically. The slow and painful process is due to begin when Pluto enters Sagittarius in 1996, and Uranus moves into Aquarius about the same time. And so the NEW AGE will begin — let us pray it is not too late!

The Aquarian Age will take over and we will see changes that affect the lives of us all, particularly people in the public eye. With Pluto's transit through Sagittarius we will find our information process completely transformed. Machines will do even more incredible things.

Slowly and deliberately, like the process of natural evolution, the economies of the world are moving together. Trading allowances and treaties will be formed which promise to become stronger than the nations which have developed them.

Social diseases may be curbed, and the cause of AIDS discovered. This won't happen in years or even decades. Progress will be slow — the Aquarian Age will last for two thousand years — and eventually we shall have spiritual and physical healing. We will band together to take better care of our natural resources, stop pollution, and create a healthier environment. Already fear of AIDS has all but abolished promiscuity. In the Aquarian Age, a whole new concept of relations may develop.

Mind-boggling? Of course. It may be shattering to some and exciting and inspiring to others. How will it affect us? It will be our choice. However, it would be wise to start thinking about it now so we will be ready for changes and surprises and make the most of them. For that is astrology — not to predict what is going to happen but to prepare us for the possibilities so we can plan accordingly.